BUSINESS BUZZWORDS

Everything You Need to Know to Speak the Lingo of the 90's

Charles B. Wendel & Elaine Svensson

American Management Association

New York • Atlanta • Boston • Chicago • Kansas City • San Francisco • Washington, D. C.
Brussels • Mexico City • Tokyo • Toronto

Library of Congress Cataloging-in-Publication Data

Wendel, Charles B.
      Business buzzwords: everything you need to know to speak the
lingo of the 90's / Charles B. Wendel and Elaine Svensson.
            p.   cm.
      Includes bibliographical references and index.
      ISBN 0–8144–7894–8
      1. Business—Dictionaries.   2. Management—Dictionaries.
3. English language—Jargon.   I. Svensson, Elaine.   II. Title.
HF1001.W46   1995
650'.03—dc20   94-47980
                                                              CIP

Printing number

10   9   8   7   6   5   4   3   2   1

Contents

To the Reader

Imagine that your senior manager has sent you a memorandum via E-mail to confirm an appointment with a management consultant. His firm has just completed the first phase of reengineering your company. For the second phase, your manager has asked you to head a task force on maximizing supplier and customer contact.

To: **Charlotte Brown, Vice President**

Subject: **Customer Reengineering Task Force**

Charlotte,

I am pleased that you agreed to head the team that will conduct Phase II of our customer reengineering project. As the owners of this process, you and the team members you select will be empowered to produce a customer franchise management strategy that can achieve zero defections.

Let's get together with the consultants Monday at 9 a.m. to discuss the competitive benchmark survey and some reverse engineering for best practices. In this atmosphere of hypercompetition, we have got to start involving both customers and suppliers in teamnets.

I will be interested in your assessment of kanbrain. A new product training strategy that takes full advantage of our information network is essential. Can you give some thought to how we are going to define core competencies?

Also, can you bring me up to speed on informationalization?

                              Regards,
                              Max

The memorandum is overflowing with buzzwords. Many of
the terms are familiar to you. Like most business executives, you
read *Business Week* and *Fortune* and skim the articles on management theory and strategy, but in all likelihood this memorandum
would send you looking for help.

What is *informationalization? empowerment? kanbrain? zero defections?* What does it mean to involve suppliers and customers as
members of *teamnets?* What is a *core competency?* Or, for that matter, *reverse engineering?*

Perhaps you have a close friend from business school who is
now a management consultant. In the event that she is running a
weekend strategy session for a major competitor, you may have
already decided to head for the nearest business bookstore, and
you are now reading our book.

This book grew out of a desire to give pressured executives an
easy-to-use reference guide. We are not offering yet another new
management theory. We will, however, provide you with straightforward definitions of the buzzwords taking their place in today's
business vocabulary. These buzzwords and phrases such as *reengineering, core competencies,* and *teamnets* will, we predict, form the
core language of on-line business communications for the next
decade.

We also intend to provide you with tools for making judgments about the value of the theories or approaches being promoted. You can then decide which buzzword is fly-by-night jargon
and which is an idea to be examined, savored, and discussed with
colleagues.

This book is divided into two parts. The first part examines
how the language of everyday business life, the words used in popular business journals and books on management theory, both illu-
minates and shapes the emerging corporate landscape. These
chapters provide a methodology that the busy executive can use to
cut through the infobog of buzzwords and arrive at the core meanings of concepts.

The first chapter examines the phenomenal explosion of business buzzwords that has occurred in the last five years. Chapter 2
takes a look at the gurus of change management who are creating
this new vocabulary and rates their priority for future reading.
Chapter 3 then provides some precepts for making value judgments about new buzzwords that you will encounter. The resulting

analysis should help dispel the frustration and confusion about the underlying management theories and shift attention to practical applications.

Finally, in Chapter 4 we give you a somewhat tongue-in-cheek formula for creating your own buzzword, a popular way to communicate that management theory that you may have been nurturing for years.

These chapters will help those individuals who track the evolution of business institutions to explore the power of language and how it is shaping our actions as we attempt to revitalize the services and manufacturing industries. At the same time, we recognize that many readers will also be searching for a practical resource to consult on buzzwords that are turning up in daily conversations and the media.

Part Two of this book, therefore, presents a reference glossary of the top management buzzwords. Along with each glossary definition we have included related terms and examples and a suggested reading list that not only covers current bestsellers but also those classic business texts published during the last twenty-five to thirty years that provided the foundation for changes now underway.

In the course of writing this book, we have looked to the future of the American corporation and at the pathway of information networks taking us there. Executives at every level in every type of business organization—from entrepreneurial start-ups to the money center banks and global players—are being asked to participate in a transformation of the business marketplace. To succeed, they must learn to talk a new language replete with terms that were not part of the business lexicon years or even months ago.

Because we focus on changes in management, we have not directly addressed the rapid proliferation of terms associated with information technology (IT). We place the debate on whether management theory is shaping IT or whether the revolution in IT is driving changes in the corporate world in the same category as chicken vs. egg. Their interdependency is primal, and the interaction is ongoing. The acronyms and emoticons used on electronic networks quickly migrate into management communications, providing graphic metaphors and shorthand phrases. We have, of course, given credit where credit is due.

Acknowledgments

Making this book required input and guidance from colleagues, editors, and friends. In particular, we thank Pat Pollino, who encouraged the concept of this book in its early stages, and Adrienne Hickey, our editor, who provided frank opinions and direct feedback.

Those intellectual leaders who create the buzzwords and are discussed in Chapter 2 provided us with inspiration. But many others from our own past and present have provided us with the intellectual leadership and encouragement that allowed us to attempt to write this book. They include David Nadler, Allan Kennedy, and Gary Helt. We thank them and our families for their support and confidence.

Part
One

1

What's in a Word?

"If words are indeed the heralds of change. . . ."

—Charles Handy, *The Age of Unreason*

Reengineering. Downsizing. Teamnets. TQM. Modern management practice has not only become a relentless cycle of self-improvement, it has also precipitated a simultaneous avalanche of new buzzwords and new phrases.

"If words are indeed the heralds of change," as Charles Handy suggests in *The Age of Unreason,* there can be no doubt that change is sweeping through the marketplace. The vocabulary used in the day-to-day business life of the 1990s is being reinvented with the same vigor and the same speed as the corporate organization itself.

In a culture where we prefer sound bytes to in-depth commentary, have an attention span molded by the fifteen-second commercial, and consider music videos art, business buzzwords are the ideal communication tools for recasting our imagery of the corporate world. Packaging the visual impact of computer graphics with the intellectual content of a special-purpose lexicon, words and phrases such as *horizontal management, rightsizing, mass customization,* and *paradigm shift* provide an intelligent interpretation of rapidly shifting market realities.

For the postindustrial organization emerging from the surgery of cost cutting and restructuring, buzzwords can help management shape its approach to the emerging marketplace. These words, such as *alliances, market-driven management,* and *servant leadership,* provide a blueprint for uniting the workforce in the pursuit of improved performance and higher productivity.

Every era adopts its own distinct vocabulary and often creates new meanings for old words, but today's crop of business buzz-words has developed an almost mesmerizing power that both evokes and fuels the dynamism of the changing corporate environment. Business buzzwords not only describe external competitive challenges but in their use have become instruments of change in the organization. By articulating the management dream and providing the metaphors that can mold the employee mind-set, buzz-words are defining the business strategies required to build the new corporate enterprise.

Like political graffiti, however, business buzzwords not only challenge but amuse or, in some cases, anger their readers and listeners. They have become highly visible, value-laden symbols of the revolution that is moving management in new directions. Rarely are we left feeling neutral when a new buzzword is coined.

Love 'em or hate 'em, the energy of buzzwords is undeniable, and the corporate renewal they broadcast is exciting.

The Message and the Media

Buzzwords provide the media pathway for "walking the talk" of the new management practices. A quick scan of the business press for buzzwords gives an immediate reading on the messages being sent to corporate America and the global marketplace.

Newspapers with as geographically diverse audiences as *The Financial Times* of London, *The Wall Street Journal,* and the Morris County *Daily Record* in central New Jersey regularly interview business school professors and consultants for explanations of management theories and explications of buzzwords. National Public Radio has run round-up stories on *downsizing* and *reengineering. Business Week,* proclaiming the advent of the *horizontal corporation,* is only one of many publications to sketch a blueprint for the new process-oriented organization structure. Mike Hammer and James Champy's book *Reengineering the Corporation* stayed on *The New York Times* bestseller list for close to a year.

The search is obviously in full swing for explanations of market phenomena and prescriptions for success. During the first seven months of 1994, for example, based on a Dow Jones News Retrieval search, the press logged 5,378 stories on empowerment and 9,598 stories on downsizing. The usage frequency for these and other concepts and their attendant buzzwords rises and falls with the popularity and acceptance, and of course the rejection, of management theories.

The word *reengineering*, as might be expected from the sales of the Hammer and Champy book, rose to prominence during the two-year span from 1992 to 1994. The word appeared 2,527 times in the press over a twenty-four-month period between July 1992 and June 1994 (Exhibit 1).

In contrast, over the same period, citations of *TQM* (total quality management) first rose slightly and then began to fall. They ranged from 523 during the last half of 1992, peaked at a high of 685 between July and December 1993, and ended the first six months of 1994 with a declining frequency of 487 occurrences, indicating that media curiosity had peaked and, even more likely, suggesting that management has moved on to new fads. Reengineering, which appears to be reaching the top of its *s-curve*, may now be headed into decline like TQM.

Exhibit 1. Occurrences of *reengineering* and *TQM* in major publications.

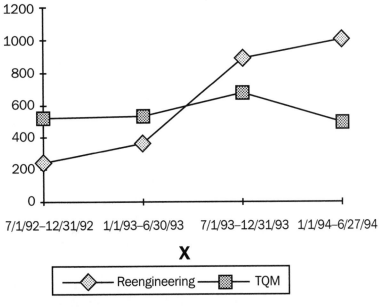

Source: Dow Jones News Retrieval.

Management's Field of Dreams

Buzzwords and the management theories they represent, of course, have a limited tryout with the corporate community. Most buzzwords pop with the intensity of a strobe flash and fade to black. To paraphrase *Fortune* magazine, there is nothing like the stench of yesterday's buzzwords.

Unless they are promoted diligently and address an immediate business need, most buzzwords are destined to fade away and become writing on the tombstones in management's field of forgotten dreams. Very often, the media focus on those words is connected with the marketing campaign for a new book, the publicity for an executive seminar, or even the advertising campaign for a management consulting firm. For example, Leveraging Core Competencies is now an executive education program at Dartmouth College's Amos Tuck School of Business Administration. *Outsourcing* and *partnering* are among the topics at a New York University course on the demands management will face in the 1990s and beyond. Advertising for Bill Creech's book *The Five Pillars of TQM* proclaims, "Give yourself the Total Quality edge."

Consulting News, a monthly periodical covering trends in management consulting, presented an overview on the life span of a buzzword (Exhibit 2).

Using *business process reengineering* (BPR) as the case example, buzzwords can be viewed as passing through five phases of popularity:

Phase 1.	*Discovery:*	A buzzword is born.
Phase 2.	*Wild acceptance:*	The idea catches fire.
Phase 3.	*Digestion:*	The concept is subject to criticism.
Phase 4.	*Disillusionment:*	The idea does not solve all problems.
Phase 5.	*Hard core:*	Only true believers remain loyal.

In mid-1994, BPR had been discovered, overcome the hurdle of initial acceptance, and moved into the digestion stage, and although still riding high was, we submit, inevitably heading toward disillusionment.

Exhibit 2. Life cycle of a management fad.

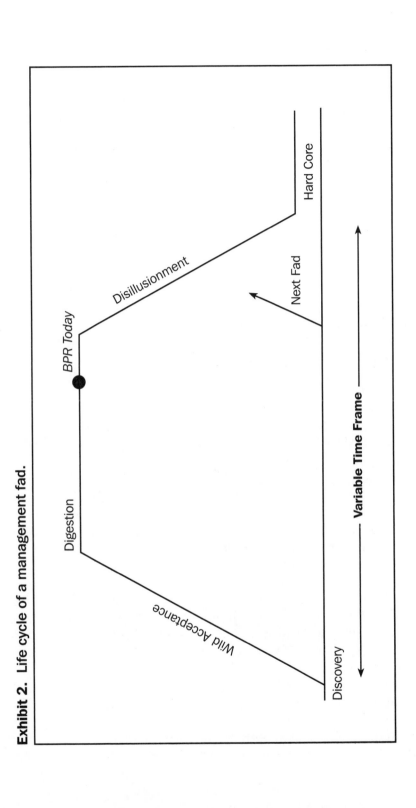

But, as one buzzword fades, the next always appears on the horizon, vying for fame. For example, by the end of 1994, *organizational architecture* and *loyalty-based management* were two terms moving into the limelight. But, entering the mainstream were concepts such as moving "beyond loyalty," whereby Tom Peters was urging employees to think of themselves and their future even as they served the corporation.

A New Corporate Mind-Set

Today's corporate managers often admit that they feel like the blind men trying to describe an elephant. The new marketplace is taking shape around them, and they are constantly looking for the words and management systems to explain the realignment of relationships with employees, customers, and even competitors.

Taking the pulse of the market, the management gurus, such as Charles Handy, Tom Peters, and Peter Drucker, actively promote the power of new words to shape the collective corporate mind. Throughout their books and articles on business theory, there are multiple references to this search for a new vocabulary that can first describe the changes underway and, perhaps even more importantly, communicate and facilitate them.

These gurus and management consulting firms freely invent new business buzzwords and view them as both verbal and marketing tools. While some admit that these words may be occasionally laughable, frequently frustrating, and always much debated, others stress that buzzwords serve a much-needed function in the debate on how to reshape the corporate enterprise.

As Peter Drucker made clear when he analyzed business life in the 1940s, and as Terrence Deal and Allan Kennedy reminded us in the 1980s, corporations do indeed create their own cultures. Corporate life is a social system with its own rules, rituals, vocabulary, and expectations for performance. The language used in management communications is, of course, the most subtle test of all. In the boardroom as well as in teenage gangs, military units, sororities, and personal relationships in the 1990s, using the politically correct lingo is an implicit test for membership.

In the late twentieth century, the corporation has become "our gang" for most Americans. It is the dominant social institution, and it lends vocabulary to a multitude of other social groups. The buzzwords describing management change, for example, are working their way into all aspects of life from religious institutions to the government and the U.S. Army. Vice President Al Gore announced programs to "reinvent government." The U.S. Army has proclaimed that it is "embracing Information Age Technology and the power of the computer to redesign itself" and build "the organization structure needed in the next century."

The use of business buzzwords signals an attempt to communicate and share a change of direction with a broad audience. In that respect, today's crop of buzzwords serves a function distinctly different from the corporate jargon that proliferates inside any organization. In contrast to buzzwords, internal jargon is a proprietary language reinforcing the boundaries of the inner circle. For example, at one consulting firm, projects for clients are called "cases." At Microsoft, intellectual and management capability is described as "bandwidth." At Coors Co., new beers are referred to as the "liquid." True corporate jargon is exclusionary, a mature dialect.

Do some buzzwords become corporate jargon? Certainly. When a management practice is integrated into a corporation's management strategy, the buzzword immediately becomes proprietary language. How else can management communicate goals and ensure that employees share the same vision for the future?

Corporate Graffiti

Buzzwords, however, get no respect. In fact, they get lots of abuse. Critics always ask: Are these new words really necessary? Aren't they symptoms of a dysfunctional corporate environment? Aren't buzzwords just corporate graffiti?

As their name implies, buzzwords do, indeed, chainsaw a pathway through rigid mind-sets and introduce intrusive management methods. Negative reactions are understandable. While words such as *reengineering* and *horizontal management* represent genuine innovations in management practice, these programs have already demonstrated their dark side, a capability to eliminate jobs and demand higher levels of responsibility and productivity from fewer employees. Buzzwords, and the concepts behind them, generally shake things up, and the management theories they represent are, without a doubt, disruptive.

Buzzwords are, therefore, often justifiably greeted with suspicion. At home in the same category as graffiti messages on subway walls and notes from hackers embedded in electronic mail systems, buzzwords can be powerful, sometimes frightening and confusing propaganda tools. To the uninitiated observer or anyone worried by potential job loss, buzzwords and acronyms such as *downsizing, BPR,* and *AVA* often appear to be splashed across the corporate landscape with subversive intentions.

The resulting reaction to buzzwords from the general public, the press, and even the management specialists is often ambiguous and, indeed, occasionally verges on anger. Try initiating a discussion of buzzwords with a management consultant or a business school professor, especially one who has not yet invented a buzzword. Chances are they will launch into criticism of the latest management fad, urge back-to-basics realism, and invent a buzzword in the process.

The columnists in the popular press focus even more specifically on the new words as the mortar shells of change. Many, if not all, headlines for the stories about buzzwords exhibit an almost palpable sense of resistance and fear. An occasional suggestion of violence even works its way into the headlines. Take, for example:

"Buzzwords Killing Common Sense in Management"
"Death by a Thousand Newfangled Buzzwords"
"Need to Keep the Change Machine Under Control"

Depending on your mood, these descriptions can verge on paranoia or sound wildly amusing. The journalists' condemnation of business-babble may make you feel as though the new business rhetoric is part of a conspiracy, either for or against capitalism.

In actuality, past the headlines, most journalists and management theorists quite sensibly criticize the use of buzzwords without the users first establishing agreed-upon definitions. The adoption of new management practices such as *downsizing,* without giving thought to the long-range consequences, is robustly condemned.

The buzzword habit, however, appears to be inescapable. For example, many critics invent new buzzwords in the process of analyzing these supposedly offensive phrases. When interviewed in *The Financial Times* about business buzzwords, Tom Robertson of the London Business School, for example, was given credit for coining "corporate graffiti." Robert Eccles and Nitin Nohria, both on the faculty at Harvard Business School, acknowledge the power of rhetoric and present an admirable analysis of its role in business communications. But, while they condemn most buzzwords as "hype," in their book *Beyond the Hype*, the two professors suggest that managers emphasize "rigorous action" rather than any one buzzword discipline. "Rigorous action" may be rhetorical meat and potatoes rather than *nouvelle cuisine*, but it is already a buzzword that we have heard used in more than one presentation by other management consultants.

This competitive hostility among consultants and management gurus is an understandable reaction. These are, after all, professionals under siege, and buzzwords represent highly prized and sought-after intellectual capital. Some organizations, in fact, confirm the power of buzzwords by laying legal and very public claim to their use. Unisys, for example, has service marked its *customerize* philosophy. One management consulting firm even attempted to claim the phrase *change management*, but the buzzword gained a life of its own and is no longer solely associated with that firm.

"Let's Talk"

Business communications skill has become an acknowledged success factor for fast-track managers. Or, should we say it has become a "core competency"? As production and marketing departments begin to redesign the infrastructure of the industrial age corporation, a communications style is evolving for managing the new knowledge workers.

The information age corporation is demanding fast, clear, and interactive communications across the electronic networks that link the new corporation. Buzzwords, in fact, facilitate this communications stream, providing a type of dialect or communications code. Just as the Gulf War spawned Hummers, World War II gave us GI Joe, and the Great Depression brought us the New Deal and the WPA, today's crop of buzzwords provides a sublanguage for business, often condensing several concepts into one image for ease of communication.

The results are compacted phrases such as *balanced scorecard* and the *learning organization,* portmanteau words such as *gainsharing, sur/petition,* or *imaginization,* and acronyms such as *TQM, BPR,* and *AVA.* This shorthand vocabulary offers a generation of managers under extreme stress in a volatile economy both new cultural and financial options plus the ability to communicate their strategies to peers and staff easily.

In fact, the use of buzzwords is likely to increase. Within the wired corporation, daily work communications are becoming increasingly informal and symbolic. As reality is built less and less through face-to-face meetings and more through electronic networks, it will become a construct in each individual's mind built on personal interpretation of words and numbers. E-mail communications and the use of workshare software will undoubtedly expand. Executives who must key in data and memoranda themselves without secretarial support will seek the mutual understandings that can be achieved through the use of a succinct, commonly held vocabulary with agreed-upon definitions.

To keep pace with the growing reliance on buzzwords, more and more consultants are preparing glossaries to bring their clients on board. Paul Allen, a management consultant who works with commercial banks, says that he makes it clear to senior management that reengineering is not in the same category as downsizing or simple cost cuts. To keep the terminology straight, he added a lexicon to his recent book *Reengineering the Bank.*

If you have any doubts about the interdependence of the new business culture and the new buzzwords, try to describe the changes already taking place in the business world without using one of the buzzwords found in the Buzzword Glossary in Part Two of this book. For example, we would ask:

Q. *How would you describe a restructured company where one manager has twenty-five direct reports?*

A. Why not try *horizontal corporation* or *open-ended management?*

Q. *How would you describe the new cooperative relationships with competitors?*

A. Some choices would be *co-opetition, co-venturing, partnership,* or *alliance.*

Q. *What performance measurement systems will be needed to evaluate the new corporate enterprise?*

A. Have you thought about *benchmarking* and *best practices* or *deaveraged profitability analysis*, followed by *activity-based accounting* as the new programs are put into effect?

Q. *How would you encourage employee creativity, making it a habit rather than a one-time exercise at an off-site seminar?*

A. What would you say to *continuous improvement? Employee empowerment?*

Q. *What values should the leaders of the new horizontal corporation follow?*

A. *Servant leadership* is an option, but what about *stewardship?*

The ability to use these buzzwords and many others in the new lexicon may, in fact, contribute to the success of managers whom corporate communications consultant Diane Gayeski calls "Renaissance Communicators." These are executives who quickly learn how to judge the value of the new management practices behind the buzzwords and become fluent in their use. In tune with the marketplace, these individuals quickly concentrate on the best ways of managing their core businesses, filtering out the business babble.

Those managers who cannot "walk the talk" may find the management track rougher going, and their corporations may fall behind competitors. Whether in writing or in face-to-face communications, the ability to use the new vocabulary of business intelligently and with a critical perspective has become one way to gain respect and status for executives within the information-age corporation.

2

Behind the Buzzwords: The Gurus of Change Management

> "Alas, every hill has a king. What is more logical than to create a hill?"
>
> —Joseph Juran, quoted in *Business Week*

Change management is a field that *The Economist* magazine described as "packed with egomaniacs and snake-oil merchants." These management consultants, business school professors, and journalists or gurus, as they are popularly called, are the buzzword kings. They can and do invent buzzwords and the accompanying theories with the speed of desktop publishing and instant books.

Are these gurus, indeed, seers who have a gifted insight into the future of business? Or, like the magicians of old, are these simply alchemists promising every manager that their buzzword is the one that will open the door to increased profits?

Seers or Charlatans?

Whether these gurus are seers or charlatans is a debate which may now have become a permanent part of the process required to validate new buzzwords and new management theories. Without a doubt, the words and the makers of buzzwords have become inseparable.

The management gurus are certainly a charismatic sect. Some seem to be constantly auditioning both in the *Harvard Business Review* and *Fortune*. Many venture on stage as stars of the after-dinner and executive seminar circuits. For example, Tom Peters, who admittedly has gifted insight into management trends, has turned himself into a virtual industry—holding seminars, selling videos, audiotapes, and of course, books—talking about buckyborgs and the de-organized corporation of the future. Although Joseph Juran was eighty-eight years old in 1993, he also demonstrated true marketing flair when, like Nolan Ryan and Billy Graham, he mounted a farewell tour, selling tickets to business executives who gladly spent the day at the feet of a master to learn the quality movement's rules of management.

It is probably wise, however, to be both a little cynical as well as excited when encountering gurus as charismatic as Juran and Peters, to name only two. Their management theories not only offer corporate managers business strategies, management philosophies, and step-by-step plans for business change, they are as tightly wrapped in a package of buzzwords as the religious doctrine of any born-again preacher.

Faced with such highly professional image marketing, how can a business manager decide which gurus to follow, which buzzwords to use, and which theories to accept? To help you build your own value tree for judging new buzzwords, this chapter offers tips for ranking the gurus.

The Scorecard

Acknowledging that most buzzwords have an extremely short half-life, we have selected close to twenty management gurus to profile. These buzzword masters—all of whom are still alive—are original writers, thinkers, and influencers developing new management methodologies and, consequently, inventing new buzzwords. All have made an active attempt to communicate their ideas to a wide audience through writing, lectures, or consulting assignments. Consequently, their works are often the source and inspiration for other gurus in the secondary ranks.

Many well-known first-tier management writers and thought leaders, of course, have never made the creation of buzzwords a priority. Marvin Bower, Ram Charan, Max DePree, Peter Drucker, and Edward Lawler, for example, are among those in that group. Other gurus such as W. Edwards Deming and Joseph Juran have contributed significantly to the theoretical base as well as to the many buzzwords currently in circulation. We have not included profiles of these gurus in the write-ups which follow, choosing instead to focus on people more directly associated with buzzword creation.

In particular Peter Drucker, although not a direct creator of buzzwords, must be acknowledged as the preeminent management thinker of the past, present, and, probably, the foreseeable future. His writings provide the intellectual foundation of many of the buzzwords discussed in this book. The concepts behind words such as *empowerment, informationalizing, paradigm shift, reengineering,* among others, can be found in his early works. Similarly, the thrust of much of Ram Charan's work appears to be based on the need for rethinking the traditional business paradigm, incorporating a frank evaluation both of existing corporate *core competencies* as well as those required for future growth.

Although we recognize the contribution of these concept makers, we have chosen to focus attention on the buzzword masters.

Take Them at Their Word

With the wisdom of age and the knowledge of what it takes to become a guru, Joseph Juran offered an excellent metaphor for the multiplication of business buzzwords and the influence of the management gurus when he commented on the popularity of *reengineering* for *Business Week.* "We have situations where some people want to be on top of a hill," Juran said. "Alas, every hill has a king. What is more logical than to create a hill?"

The marketing of a new management theory such as reengineering certainly has parallels to Moses when he delivered the Ten Commandments from the mount. Prestige and recognition for business gurus has become so closely tied to coining a new buzzword that it is hard to find a popular guru without a buzzword.

If business gurus can find the right "hill" to climb, they automatically have a podium from which they can proclaim a vision. Charles Handy, for example, proclaims *shamrock management;* Philip Crosby describes *completeness;* Tom Peters talks about *de-organized* corporations. The list could go on.

Although not discussed in this chapter, Faith Popcorn may provide the best example of this in-your-face type of marketing savvy. She has made a successful business selling an early warning system to business executives who try to anticipate the popular consequences of *paradigm shifts.* Even her catchy name, adopted later in life, serves as a buzzword representing a fun and palatable idea popping into consciousness from a small seed ignored by many as a dull kernel.

A majority of these synthetically produced phrases, of course, represent sincere attempts to communicate complex ideas to readers and listeners, quickly and without elaborate explanations. If that word becomes a household as well as an office buzzword, so much the better. The bestseller lists and talk shows beckon.

Positioning the Gurus

Because the buzzword gurus operate in their own intellectual galaxy, it is possible to position this group on a matrix according to their philosophical and practical leanings. In Exhibit 3 the best-known gurus are positioned in one of four quadrants. The x-axis on this matrix reflects the extent to which the business expert is a practical realist versus philosopher. The y-axis assesses the viability of the near-term solutions they propose versus their focus on the intangible or ideal solution.

Those gurus who classify as realists, such as the teams of Hamel and Prahalad and Hammer and Champy, concentrate on the actual tactical and strategic problems facing managers, such as growth and restructuring. They also propose solutions which, although not painless, can be implemented or, at least, begun in the near term. In contrast, management philosophers such as Charles Handy often choose the big-picture approach. They see the corporate world as a microcosm that reflects the larger universe of social issues ranging from education to government. The ideas of these philosophers certainly help explain trends and put phenomena in context, but rarely do these gurus offer solutions that will

Exhibit 3. Buzzwords gurus: spheres of influence.

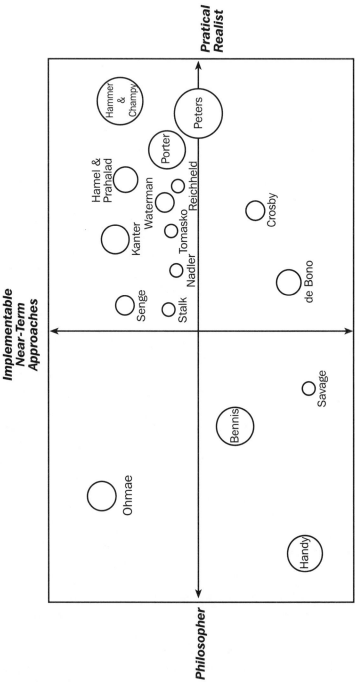

help run a day-to-day business. A few theorists, such as Peter Senge, develop big-picture theories and follow up with practical workbooks that present both tools and strategies.

Often those theorists who boast the most seductive buzzwords concentrate on emerging social and political trends that may not see a practical application for another five to ten years. But buzzwords, of course, are found across the entire spectrum of management theory.

Although each of the gurus profiled is frequently included in roundups of leading-edge thinkers, each one's sphere of influence varies. The size of his or her circle on this matrix provides a subjective view of his or her current relative position in the marketplace. Tom Peters, Mike Hammer, and James Champy, for example, currently have greater popular impact than Charles Savage. These spheres are also not static. For example, Gary Hamel and C. K. Prahalad's visibility and influence are expanding whereas others may be at the outer limits of their fifteen minutes of fame. Those with the smallest circles of influence today could be the stars of the future.

To assist you in building your own value structure, it is helpful to take a look at each of these gurus in more depth. We have provided a summary of their contribution to management theory, a list of their key works and signature phrases. For those readers who have limited time but may wish to pursue further study, we have also provided a priority ranking for each guru of low, medium, or high.

Warren Bennis

How to be a leader in the new organization taking shape is certainly the hottest topic in the executive suite, and Warren Bennis is the foremost guru to consult.

Bennis provides a framework that models the role of leaders. He states that effective leaders never look back, demonstrating what he calls the Wallenda Factor. These people "overlook error and constantly embrace positive goals." Bennis identifies four management competencies in every successful leader:

1. *Management of attention.* The ability to communicate and attract others

2. *Management of meaning.* The ability to use metaphors to make an idea tangible
3. *Management of trust.* A function of the individual's reliability and constancy
4. *Management of self.* Knowing one's own skills and using them effectively

Although Bennis does not focus on the practical difficulties of introducing change within a company, he does sketch the big picture. He defines empowerment of the workforce as the collective effect of leadership and envisions an organization where learning is encouraged, honest failure accepted, and a sense of community exists.

Growth and leadership require an organization theory or "social architecture" that is "capable of creating intellectual capital . . . ideas, know-how, innovation, brains, knowledge, and expertise." Bennis identifies this capability as one of the keys to the future because "you cannot restructure or reengineer your company into prosperity."

In line with this vision of leadership, Bennis has promoted federalism, where a large company achieves revitalization by being reformed into a collection of smaller companies.

Key works:	*Leaders: The Strategies for Taking Charge* with Burt Nanus (1985) *On Becoming a Leader* (1989) *An Invented Life: Reflections on Leadership and Change* (1993)
Signature phrases:	empowerment, federalism, intellectual capital, learning organization, social architecture, Wallenda Factor
Priority:	High for executives building their own leadership skills or those professionals involved in executive training programs.

Philip Crosby

Crosby's company, Philip Crosby Associates, has done much to promote the quality revolution and *TQM*, two buzzwords that now appear to be on the downward spiral of popularity. Crosby emphasizes that high quality can be maintained best by preventing errors from occurring. He is, in effect, a contemporary spokesperson for W. Edwards Deming's theories.

In his latest book, *Completeness,* Crosby states, "Quality (meaning getting everyone to do what they have agreed to do) is the skeletal structure of an organization; finance is the nourishment; and relationships are the soul. All of this comes together in what I call *Completeness."*

Crosby names those who will make completeness happen *centurions.* On his scalar, these are the corporate leaders who will break down internal organizational barriers and make certain that the customer is well served.

In essence this doctrine of completeness appears to be an attempt to reposition the TQM movement which has been, at best, a partial success. Whereas *Quality Is Free* can be considered a detailed road map for instituting a quality program, *Completeness* focuses only on the philosophy.

Key works:	*Quality Is Free: The Art of Making Quality Certain* (1979)
	Completeness: Quality for the 21st Century (1994)
Signature phrases:	centurions, completeness
Priority:	Low, unless you are a TQM junkie.

Edward de Bono

The buzzword *lateral thinking* is one among several created and popularized by de Bono, who admits that he likes to write books on long plane flights using a laptop computer, an excellent metaphor for the fast-moving world of management theory and the creation of buzzwords.

In her book *Instant Management,* Carol Kennedy characterizes de Bono as "the foremost example of a guru who has built a reputation out of one 'Big Idea.' "

That idea is lateral thinking, which de Bono sees as involving "the generation of new ideas and the escape from old ones." In effect lateral thinking employs techniques of discontinuity, such as the use of analogy and random word association games to break away from traditional patterns of thought.

De Bono has developed numerous seminars from this idea as well as several books. *Six Thinking Hats* uses the device of changing hats color coded to different states of mind, first physically and then mentally, to understand different perspectives and mind-sets. His latest book *Sur/petition,* in addition to inventing an extraordinary buzzword, applies these ideas to service and competition to motivate a company to go the extra mile to serve the customer.

Key works:	*Lateral Thinking for Management* (1971)
	Atlas of Management Thinking (1983)
	Six Thinking Hats (1985)
	Sur/petition (1992)
Signature phrases:	discontinuity, lateral thinking, six thinking hats, sur/petition
Priority:	Medium to Low. Other writers offer more accessible approaches for encouraging outside-the-box thinking.

Gary Hamel and C. K. Prahalad

The signature phrases introduced by Gary Hamel and C. K. Prahalad have become mandatory buzzwords in today's business vocabulary.

The concepts behind *core competencies,* for example, are the basis for much contemporary business thought. Hamel and Prahalad, both business school professors, have explored the concept of core competencies within a corporation, that is, its "collective learning," which creates a competitive advantage by "harmonizing streams of technology . . . the organization of work, and the delivery of value." In their view companies possess no more than five or six fundamental competencies. These competencies "make a disproportionate contribution to customer-perceived value," are "competitively unique," and can be applied to various product areas.

Recognizing that core competencies are the lifeblood of a corporation, Hamel and Prahalad proceed to explore the corpus. They have created the concept of *strategic architecture,* a buzzword that communicates the business system and the infrastructure that can exploit core competencies to create core products and produce end products that can be sold into the marketplace. These two gurus recognize the conflict between fragmented, decentralized organizational structures, such as those based on the strategic business unit (SBU), and the more holistic architecture required to achieve an organization's potential.

In their view growth depends in part on taking a leadership role by emphasizing industry foresight that, in turn, requires creating "hindsight in advance." Therefore, they not only focus on evaluating a company's current core competencies but also stress the need for management to agree both on the competencies required for growth and the path for acquiring those capabilities.

Key works:	"Strategic Intent," *Harvard Business Review* (May–June 1989) "The Core Competence of the Corporation," *Harvard Business Review* (May–June 1990) *Competing for the Future: Breakthrough Strategies for Seizing Control of Your Industry and Creating the Markets of Tomorrow* (1994)
Signature phrases:	collective learning, competitive innovation, core competencies, core products, denominator management, industry foresight, numerator management, opportunity horizon, strategic architecture
Priority:	High. Concepts for executives who are undertaking a restructuring, renewal, or growth project.

Michael Hammer and James Champy

Hammer and Champy may not be one person but together they packaged *reengineering*—the buzzword that has ridden the crest of change management. Although they did not invent this buzzword, they have been responsible for its popularity, making it the manifesto for modern management that their book jacket proclaims.

Reengineering the Corporation has had the greatest impact of any business book since Tom Peters and Robert Waterman's *In*

Search of Excellence. The book provides a detailed understanding of reengineering, which Hammer and Champy define as "the fundamental rethinking and radical redesign of business processes to achieve dramatic improvements in critical, contemporary measures of performance, such as cost, quality, service, and speed."

Understanding reengineering as Hammer and Champy define it is a key to many other buzzword definitions. They are well aware that old-fashioned cost reduction frequently masks itself as reengineering. Successful reengineering is not *TQM* nor is it *participative management* or *downsizing.* Reengineering does, however, incorporate and expand many of these and other leading-edge concepts. This "manifesto for business revolution" is meant to prepare corporate America for future growth. When done correctly and with top management's commitment, reengineering can revitalize a company, encouraging and demanding new ways of thinking.

Hammer and Champy also recognize, however, that reengineering exercises often fail to create fundamental change or produce only mediocre results: "50 percent to 70 percent of the organizations that undertake a reengineering effort do not achieve the dramatic results they intended." Among the reasons listed for this failure are: trying to fix a process instead of changing it; not focusing on business processes; and, management being willing to settle for minor results.

Key works:	"Obliterate Don't Automate," *Harvard Business Review* (July–August 1990), pp. 104–112
	Reengineering the Corporation (1993)
	Beyond Reengineering (Hammer) (1995)
Signature phrase:	reengineering
Priority:	High. Essential competitive information.

Charles Handy

Sometimes we think Charles Handy is writing moral philosophy rather than management theory. Like Adam Smith, who was first of all a moral philosopher and only secondly an economist, Handy, who was once a petroleum executive, has now become a business moralist attempting to make sense of the confusion of modern life.

The Gods of Management (1978), Handy's first well-known book, presents the view that organizations fall into one of four categories of cultures, each represented by a Greek god: Zeus (the entrepreneurial company with strong leadership), Apollo (bureaucratic business cultures such as insurance companies), Athena (the team-based company such as a consulting firm that focuses on projects), and Dionysius (the organization that exists to help individuals such as doctors and lawyers achieve a purpose).

In his 1989 book *The Age of Unreason,* Handy describes another model for the organization and society of the future that incorporates discontinuous change. He emphasizes that the rapid changes that began occurring in the 1980s are following unfamiliar patterns that cannot necessarily be modeled or otherwise anticipated. To address these complex changes, he suggests that managers engage in upside-down thinking to recreate the external environment inside their organization.

In *The Age of Paradox* (1994) Handy consolidates his ideas about social roles, education, and management strategy that have been presented in previous publications. Becoming a guru in the classical sense of the title, he builds a rational framework intended for both organizations and individuals to use to "examine the place and meaning of business in our societies."

Handy almost appears to express guilt at his past prescience in predicting the new order now taking shape and admits that he found himself "unsettled" by the resulting confusion generated by change. His doubt is, in fact, both charming and empathic. Handy portrays himself as one of us, a family man, a businessman who has watched as well as made changes happen.

With this worldview and with certainty, Handy looks to the future. He predicts that as managers find the time to step back from the bombardment of change, more and more will begin to anticipate and preempt the "second curve," a buzzword he uses to describes what is also known as the s-curve, the natural upswing and mature downswing of any enterprise.

Key works:	*The Gods of Management* (1978)
	The Age of Unreason (1989)
	The Age of Paradox (1994)
Signature phrases:	discontinuous change, doughnut or-

	ganization, shamrock organization, second curve, upside-down thinking
Priority:	Low for practical near-term business applications. High for outside-the-box thinking and social consciousness.

Rosabeth Moss Kanter

Rosabeth Moss Kanter, former editor of the *Harvard Business Review*, Harvard University professor, and consultant, has written some of the most highly praised business books of the past two decades, and her buzzword phrase, *the change masters*, has become common parlance.

In *The Change Masters*, written in 1983, she centers on the need for participative management to ensure that individuals feel empowered and take on increased responsibility. *When Giants Learn to Dance* continued the examination of *change management*. She anticipates later work on the *virtual corporation*, presenting an acronym, *PAL*—Pool resources with others, Ally to exploit opportunities, or Link systems in partnership—to suggest that approach. Customers, suppliers, corporate management, and union and nonunion employees can cooperate and coordinate their requirements under this model.

Post-entrepreneurialism, another concept Kanter explores, has linkages to the flattened hierarchy of the horizontal corporation, whereby managers are partners, not bosses. In the worldview Kanter creates, traditional hierarchical structure is broken, and pay-for-performance incentive compensation becomes a reality.

In Kanter's most recent book (1994), the "Big Three Model" of change, codeveloped with Barry Stein and Todd Jick, is used to explore how corporations operate. This model focuses on "the forces, both external and internal, that set events in motion; the major kinds of change that correspond to each of the external and internal change pressures; and the principal tasks involved in managing the change process."

Kanter has drawn on her academic and consulting experience to provide readers with a sophisticated perspective on change. Her signature buzzwords have also provided the signposts for the road map that many other management theorists have followed.

Key works: *The Change Masters: Corporate Entrepreneurs at Work* (1983)
                      When Giants Learn to Dance (1989)
                      The Challenge of Organizational Change (1992) with Barry Stein and Todd Jick
                      "Collaborative Advantage: The Art of Alliances," *Harvard Business Review* (July–August 1994), pp. 96–108
Signature phrases: Big Three Model of organizational change, change masters, post-entrepreneurial corporation, empowerment, PAL
Priority: Medium to High

David Nadler

Nadler believes that sustaining a competitive advantage results from what he terms *organizational capability,* "the ability of the organization to innovate, to motivate, to satisfy customers." He discusses organizational architecture as the need to rethink the design of individual work units within a company as well as the design or architecture of the entire company and the relationship among companies, which he terms *interenterprise relations.*

Nadler believes that rethinking the traditional structure of an organization can result in corporate decomposition. The traditional bureaucracy will give way to an empowered workforce where you will find autonomous workers and high-performance work systems.

Nadler's vision of the corporation includes some themes being promoted by other management experts. His architecture metaphor encompasses empowered workers, the new role of management, technology-based opportunities, and both the learning and the virtual corporation. A sometime academic and founder of a well-known consulting firm, Delta Consulting, Nadler's personal strength as a thinker builds off an ability to synthesize much of what is being discussed today by other theorists with his real-life experiences working with senior corporate managers who are actively pursuing change.

Key works: *Organizational Architecture* with Marc S. Gerstein and Robert B. Shaw (1992)

	Prophets in the Dark with David T. Kearns (1992)
	Interview by A. J. Vogl with Nadler in *Across the Board* (October 1993), pp. 27–32
	Organizational Change (1994)
Signature phrases:	organizational architecture, corporate decomposition, high-performance work systems, interenterprise relations
Priority:	Medium to High

Kenichi Ohmae

They call him "Mr. Strategy" in Japan where he headed the office of McKinsey & Company. Although in recent years he has focused more on geopolitics than on profitability improvement and organizational effectiveness, one early study is considered a business masterpiece. *The Mind of the Strategist* was Ohmae's first book published in English, after five books on strategy, three of which were bestsellers in Japan. More than a decade later you will still find this dog-eared and annotated book somewhere near the desks of many top-level management consultants. First subtitled "The Art of Japanese Business" and later "Business Planning for Competitive Advantage," this management treatise stresses the "habit of analysis," the "intellectual elasticity" required to come up with "realistic responses to changing situations." It provides a rigorous approach for thinking about a business and positioning it for the future.

In his 1985 book, *Triad Power,* Ohmae focuses on the emerging global marketplace and the need for companies to develop relationships that cut across what he calls the geographic triad: the United States, Europe, and Japan. In his view, companies that seek to compete globally must become insiders in their nonindigenous areas to success. He writes, "If you are not an 'insider' in a country important to your share growth, you may find the doors to its markets tightly closed."

Key works:	*The Mind of the Strategist* (1982)
	Triad Power (1985)
	The Borderless World (1990)

Signature phrases: borderless world, insiderization, triad power

Priority: High, in particular for Ohmae's 1982 book. You can't find a bigger picture approach to strategy that also recognizes the practical exigencies of running a business.

Tom Peters

When it comes to charisma and influence, Tom Peters has it all. A former White House advisor, ex-McKinsey principal, founder of The Tom Peters Group, and a visiting scholar at the Amos Tuck School of Business Administration at Dartmouth College, Peters has not only hosted public television programs but has also appeared as a guest on *The Wall Street Journal Report* as well as many other television business-news programs.

Peters started on this fast track in pursuit of every consultant's dream of success when he coauthored *In Search of Excellence* with Robert H. Waterman, Jr. The management book was a *New York Times* bestseller for over two years and coined *excellence*, which remains a classic buzzword for top-level performance a decade later. True, the companies that Peters profiled proved that excellence was not a permanent state, but that transience gave Peters fodder for his subsequent management books *Thriving on Chaos* and *Liberation Management: Necessary Disorganization for the Nanosecond Nineties.*

Although Peters may occasionally seem like a TV evangelist when he commands the stage, his perspective is timely and important. He is also one of the few writers on management to explore both sides of a question and admit that earlier opinions may have been wrong or incomplete.

One way in which Peters differentiates his ideas is to provide readers with multiple anecdotes. In his most recent works Peters has focused on the need to abandon the past rather than change it. This break requires going *beyond* many of the popular practices that other buzzword theorists promote, including *decentralization, empowerment, company loyalty,* and *TQM.* Peters's ideas encompass models for the organization, which he says needs to become disembodied or what he calls *de-organized*, with employees going beyond loyalty, constantly thinking of personal achievement and positioning themselves for the next job.

He can be a gadfly, but Peters is never far off target or boring. He presents abstract and challenging concepts in a popular and accessible style. He prods and pushes management to rethink traditional practices.

Key works:	*In Search of Excellence* with Robert H. Waterman, Jr. (1982)
	A Passion for Excellence with Nancy Austin (1985)
	Thriving on Chaos (1987)
	Liberation Management (1992)
	The Tom Peters Seminar (1994)
Signature phrases:	excellence, beyond loyalty, bucky-borgs, de-organized, disembodied enterprise
Priority:	High. The combination of high energy ideas and real-life examples is an excellent motivation.

Michael Porter

Michael Porter has worked to apply economics to the study of management and is not shy about promoting himself as a guru. A Harvard Business School professor and a leading consultant, Porter has a worldwide reputation as a strategic thinker who takes the theoretical and presents it in practical terms that can build a pathway toward implementation. *The Competitive Advantage of Nations,* his 1990 book, which discusses how to assess a company and position it in a dynamic global marketplace, has become required reading in business schools.

Porter's second book (*Competitive Advantage,* 1985) promotes an approach termed the *value chain,* which has become a standard way of looking at a business as a system to determine its competitive advantage. In Porter's words: "Every firm is a collection of activities that are performed to design, produce, market, deliver, and support its product. All these activities can be represented using a value chain." Effective value-chain analysis includes examining the key elements driving a company's success, evaluating the interaction between those key elements, and assessing the value chains for both buyers and competitors.

Key works:	*Competitive Strategy* (1980)
	Competitive Advantage (1985)
	The Competitive Advantage of Nations (1990)
Signature phrases:	competitive advantage, competitive strategy, national competitiveness, value chain
Priority:	High

C. K. Prahalad

See Gary Hamel and C. K. Prahalad.

Frederick Reichheld

Frederick Reichheld of Bain & Co. and Earl Sasser, a Harvard Business School professor, have published a seminal article on customer retention. Reichheld has developed these ideas further in a book scheduled for publication in spring 1996.

In their view a company should aim for zero defections in its current customer base—that is, keep every customer that can be served profitably. Their *Harvard Business Review* article focuses on the economic impact of reducing defections and the outsized attractiveness of multiyear customers. They cite one example in which MBNA, the credit card company, reduced its defection rate by 10 percent, which led to a profit increase of 125 percent.

Zero defections and building off a loyal customer base can be a foundation for sustaining profitability and generating growth and, therefore, merits considerable attention. However, a customer retention program, such as the one Reichheld suggests, demands a companywide focus on understanding deaveraged profitability and/or shareholder value generated by a customer. This awareness will ensure that only those customers who create value for the company are actively serviced and retained.

Key works:	"Zero Defections: Quality Comes to Services," *Harvard Business Review*

(September–October 1990),
pp. 105–111 (with Earl W. Sasser, Jr.)

Signature phrases: loyalty-based management, zero defections

Priority: Medium. Very useful for integrating customer service management into longer-term strategy.

Charles Savage

The evolution of computer technology gives Charles Savage both a metaphor and a structure for organizational development. Savage contends that organizations have failed to gain full value from either third, fourth, or fifth generation computer technology, that is, respectively, the integrated circuit, large scale integration, and parallel networked processing units. Instead of embracing fifth generation management, as Savage describes human networking, companies have continued to manage with steep vertical hierarchies. These human bureaucracies like computer networks control the dissemination of information and consequently limit the performance of both machines and people. Savage asks an essential question, "How are we to respond to the growing chasm between our technological capabilities and organizational lethargy?"

By using the analogy of technology and stressing that it should be the tool of management, Savage has anticipated many of the organizational issues now receiving intense focus, among them how to create a virtual corporation, the achievement of productivity through employee empowerment, and the reengineering of the corporation. Unfortunately his abstract, scientific presentation style limits the effectiveness of his message. Casual readers with no technology background will find educational hurdles to overcome before they can glean the gems that *Fifth Generation Management* contains.

Key works: *Fifth Generation Management* (1990)

Signature phrases: fifth generation management, human networking, virtual enterprises

Priority: Low to Medium

Peter Senge

A member of the MIT faculty, Peter Senge is a bona fide academic and consultant/seminar leader who is exploring the leading edge of information age management theory and practice. His primary topic is the interaction between computers and management practices.

Senge identifies the need for companies to become learning organizations. By his definition, these are "organizations where people continually expand their capacity to create the results they truly desire, where new and expansive patterns of thinking are nurtured, where collective aspiration is set free, and where people are continually learning together." The organizations that will excel in the future, Senge believes, will be those that discover how to tap people's commitment and capacity to learn at all levels in an organization. Such organizations will share a corporate vision and a commitment to personal mastery that can provide a solid foundation for management practices.

As discussed in the Buzzword Glossary that follows, creating a learning organization requires five disciplines or what Senge terms *component technologies.* He mentions that, ultimately, there may be a sixth discipline required although it is currently unknown. His point is that we are dealing with a constantly evolving environment and what works today must change to meet future requirements.

Key works:	*The Fifth Discipline* (1990)
	The Fifth Discipline Fieldbook (1994)
	with Charlotte Roberts, Richard B.
	Ross, Bryan J. Smith, and Art Kleiner
Signature phrases:	fifth discipline, learning organization,
	team learning
Priority:	High

George Stalk

Stalk, a consultant at the Boston Consulting Group, is one of the gurus who concentrates on growth and competition. His focus is the importance of time as a source of competitive advantage in today's fast-moving marketplace. Reacting to the ability of the Japanese to create and move products to markets quickly, Stalk evaluated companies that compete with flexible manufacturing and rapid response systems. He arrived at the view that "by reducing the consumption of time in every aspect of the business, these companies also reduce costs, improve quality, and stay close to their customers."

Stalk's work complements concepts of reengineering, but he does not go as far as some other gurus in providing a how-to approach or in anticipating the practical difficulties that introducing the level of changes he suggests can create.

Key works:	"Time—The Next Source of Competitive Advantage," *Harvard Business Review* (July–August 1988), pp. 41–51; *Competing Against Time: How Time-based Competition Is Reshaping Global Markets* (1990) with Thomas M. Hout "Competing on Capabilities: The New Rules of Corporate Strategy," with Philip Evans and Lawrence E. Schulman, *Harvard Business Review* (March–April 1992), pp. 57–69
Signature phrase:	time-based competition
Priority:	Low to Medium

Robert M. Tomasko

While Robert M. Tomasko's solutions are based on solid management theory, they are also eminently practical and achievable. Tomasko, a consultant to Arthur D. Little, wrote one of the best books on downsizing. In it he incorporated a discussion of activity value analysis (AVA) with other initiatives, including concepts of management and workforce involvement that have come to be known as *horizontal management* and *empowerment*.

His second work moves toward a fundamental rethinking of the corporation. Tomasko envisions restructuring the organization horizontally and around business processes rather than functions. Reshaping the organization includes what he calls *information partnerships,* which stress the need of joint ventures. The book also attacks the notion of vertical hierarchy.

For example, in Tomasko's vision of the new corporation, the middle manager will have a positive impact, setting direction, providing support to employees, and measuring results. Rethinking the corporation means that roles and responsibilities will change; static jobs will become dynamic assignments; staff areas will be more closely linked to line needs. The new organization will be piloted by managers who will share their power with professional workers on a nonmanagement track.

Tomasko's metaphorical shape for the organization of the future is the dome rather than the pyramid. He says, "[Domes] are very efficient configurations because they are extremely thin compared to the distances they span. If an arch-shaped structure, or pyramid, were to cover the same space as a dome, it would have to be ten times as thick to support itself."

Key works:	*Downsizing: Reshaping the Corporation for the Future* (1990) *Rethinking the Corporation: The Architecture of Change* (1993)
Signature phrases:	demassing, downsize, information partnerships, resize, reshape
Priority:	Medium to High

Robert Waterman

Ever since his landmark examination of excellent companies, *In Search of Excellence,* with Tom Peters, Robert Waterman has chosen to concentrate on the circumstances that companies require to recreate themselves to stay on top or to stay competitive. For Waterman, those companies that are successful exemplify eight themes:

1. Informed optimism
2. Clear direction and companywide empowerment
3. Reliance on accessible facts and congenial controls
4. The ability to anticipate crisis
5. Teamwork and trust
6. The habit of habit breaking
7. Positive attitudes and attention exhibited by management
8. A focus on the individual's commitment to fulfilling corporate goals

Waterman's vision complements the proponents of an organization based on mass customization. Organizational flexibility and the willingness to recreate the company regularly allow management to respond to changes in its competitive marketplace.

Waterman cites Warren Bennis and Alvin Toffler for previously developing one of the most popular buzzword terms currently in use, *adhocracy*. He quotes Bennis for articulating the need for "adaptive problem solving, temporary systems of diverse specialists linked together . . . in an organized flux."

For Waterman, developing high-performance teams seems to be the answer to creating a flexible, market-responsive organization. The type of teaming that he recommends also requires what is, in effect, corporate reengineering.

Key works:	*In Search of Excellence* with Tom Peters (1982)
	The Renewal Factor (1987)
	Adhocracy (1992)
	What America Does Right: Learning from Companies That Put People First (1994)
Signature phrases:	adhocracy, excellence, renewal factor
Priority:	Low to Medium

3

Value Judgments

"How do you know high value work when you see it?"

—Robert M. Tomasko, *Rethinking the Corporation*

How do you react when you encounter a new buzzword? With disdain? Do you admit your perplexity? Ask for a definition? Act knowledgeable and tough it out? How can you know, as Robert Tomasko asked, high value work when you see it?

New business buzzwords emerge every week. Some are generic, whereas others are industry or market specific. A few, such as *quality management,* not only appear to be applicable to every company but also capture the popular imagination.

Taking the purist approach and bemoaning the fate of the English language is, of course, one answer. Buzzwords do confuse. They certainly are a type of jargon, and many of us have at least had a good laugh if not shed a few tears over confusing memorandums and manuals overflowing with trendy metaphors. Some employees have even had to pay for the privilege of using buzzwords. One group at AlliedSignal suffered a one dollar fine, payable whenever a buzzword was used.

But being either punitive or high-minded is not always productive, particularly in the charged political atmosphere of a corporate restructuring or on a potentially lucrative sales call, both instances where buzzwords often set the tone and define the action.

In fact, this book has been written partially in response to the frustration expressed by one corporate executive who wanted to keep pace with his peers. Several months ago when we visited the president of a successful New York Stock Exchange-listed company with headquarters in a major western city, he was full of questions about buzzwords. Our meeting took place shortly after a casual conversation he had with several colleagues who served with him on the same board of directors.

Two of his fellow executives had started a discussion of the Hammer and Champy book on *reengineering*. They gave examples of their companies' reengineering strategies. One talked about using *benchmarking* and *best practices* as ways to transform his company. Another talked about identifying and focusing on *core competencies*. A third discussed *breakpoint analysis* and *paradigm shifts*.

During our meeting, our client's questions were direct. He asked, "What exactly is *reengineering?* How does it differ from cost reduction? Why should I try it?"

Numerous other questions followed, including, "Do you think *benchmarking* really has value for a company in my industry niche? What do management consultants mean by *breakpoint analysis?*"

This string of questions made us realize that buzzwords, like popcorn, are exploding in the business consciousness. But, although these words are liberally used, they are rarely defined by the users who themselves may not know the textbook definition. It was also clear that if this company president, who has an MBA and thirty years' line experience, could not immediately identify the management theories being promoted by these buzzwords, then thousands of other executives were facing the same challenge.

Given the plethora of buzzwords and the word-creation machine being fed daily by management gurus trying to create their own hill, how can the average, harried executive sift through fads and ineffective panacea to keep current with important new ideas? Who can possibly read every management text or manage total recall on the concepts behind all the metaphors and snappy imagery?

Five Questions to Ask

Whether it happens in causal conversation with a customer, while reading an E-mail memorandum, or in a debate with a senior manager, never-before-heard buzzwords are certain to appear. Rather than being caught unprepared and confused, you can develop a strategy for responding to these emerging buzzwords, a way to assess their value.

By value we mean applicability to a business scenario or management situation. For example, neither *reengineering* nor *adhocracy* is appropriate for all companies. Conversely, some buzzwords, such as *benchmarking* and *best practices,* offer a perspective on performance measurement that could become a building block for many.

We suggest asking five questions to categorize and judge the value and usefulness of the management system or theory that a buzzword represents. The next time a buzzword does not register immediately, try asking:

1. Does this buzzword ring a bell?
2. Does the buzzword suggest ways to evaluate business operations?
3. Does the buzzword focus on performance improvement?
4. Is the buzzword linked to strategies for growth?
5. Does the buzzword represent a new approach to management?

By asking these questions and weighing the answers against a company's internal objectives, any executive worth his or her salt can quickly judge the value behind a buzzword and prioritize its importance for future investigation.

Question 1: Does This Buzzword Ring a Bell?

Much of the mystique and power of management buzzwords results from the fact that they are an unknown quantity. Even so, many words will ring bells, and the similarities will become apparent when the theories inspiring them are compared.

When encountering a new buzzword, the first step, therefore, should be to check its lineage. In reality, very few buzzwords reinvent the wheel. Most repackage concepts that may have been discussed back in the 1940s and 1950s when corporations were first being analyzed as social systems. Most notably, a review of Peter Drucker's work will reveal the roots of many buzzwords.

Because management theory has assumed the structure and trappings of a science over the intervening years, many of these concepts are routinely reexamined and repackaged, often with the same fanfare as a totally new concept. One excellent example of the repeated rediscovery of a management theory is the evolution of *paradigm* as a buzzword.

As Exhibit 4 demonstrates, the information superhighway that links Joel Barker's *Paradigms*, Don Tapscott and Art Caston's *Paradigm Shift*, and Tom Peters and Robert Waterman's *In Search of Excellence* to Gary Hamel and C. K. Prahalad's *Competing for the Future* is a well-marked route. These management texts share a common history, and each owes considerable intellectual debt along the way to the writings of Edward de Bono, Thomas Kuhn, and, of course, Peter Drucker, the father of modern management theory, who started it all.

Business buzzwords, such as *paradigm*, will continue to multiply and mutate. We will consider this book a success, however, if the next time readers hear a new buzzword they don't hesitate to ask, "Isn't that a lot like. . . ?" Executives who develop a sense of management history are the best positioned to cut through the buzzword haze, exercise value judgments, and gain maximum usefulness from any new business buzzword.

Question 2: Does the Buzzword Suggest Ways to Evaluate Business Operations?

Many of the buzzwords being promoted by consultants and business school professors represent management tools for the measurement and evaluation of current profitability.

Together, the best of these buzzwords provide the chapter headings in a management primer for evaluating performance. They are a basic tool kit for prioritizing marketing and investment initiatives.

Even when buzzwords are developed by different theorists, the tools they represent can produce a database on how well a business is currently operating. They can also give management a road map of improvements in today's information-age marketplace. Buzzwords that help evaluate business operations, therefore, fall into three categories:

1. *Evaluation of competitors' strategies.* Surveys of direct competitors as well as companies that are well known for a particular skill such as customer service or product innovation can provide a company with standards for judging their current operations.

Exhibit 4. Evolution of *paradigm* as a buzzword.

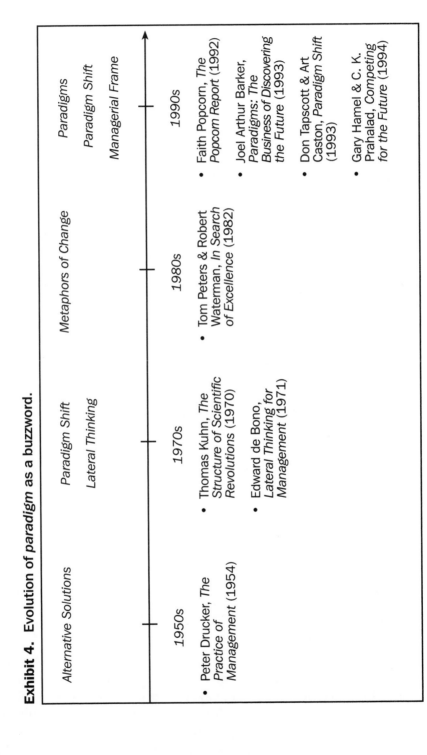

Alternative Solutions	*Paradigm Shift*	*Metaphors of Change*	*Paradigms*
	Lateral Thinking		*Paradigm Shift*
			Managerial Frame
1950s	*1970s*	*1980s*	*1990s*
• Peter Drucker, *The Practice of Management* (1954)	• Thomas Kuhn, *The Structure of Scientific Revolutions* (1970) • Edward de Bono, *Lateral Thinking for Management* (1971)	• Tom Peters & Robert Waterman, *In Search of Excellence* (1982)	• Faith Popcorn, *The Popcorn Report* (1992) • Joel Arthur Barker, *Paradigms: The Business of Discovering the Future* (1993) • Don Tapscott & Art Caston, *Paradigm Shift* (1993) • Gary Hamel & C. K. Prahalad, *Competing for the Future* (1994)

Some buzzwords in this category are *balanced scorecard, benchmarking, best practices, reverse engineering,* and *valufacture.*

2. *Financial assessment of performance.* The foundation of any performance improvement or management innovation starts with a number-based assessment of performance. The primary buzzword in this category is *deaveraged profitability analysis.*

3. *Shareholder interests.* A commitment to the best interest of owners of the company belongs at the top of every senior manager's agenda. The buzzwords in this category are related to financial assessment but emphasize the economic worth of a product, business, or customer to the shareholder. Among the buzzwords are *economic value added (EVA), shareholder value analysis (SVA), value creators,* and *value destroyers.*

Question 3: Does the Buzzword Focus on Performance Improvement?

Performance improvement activities are based on an analytical understanding of current operations, and the associated buzzwords are, most often, linked with programs that focus largely, but not exclusively, on cost reduction. These buzzwords derive largely from the terminology of management systems that became popular in the late 1980s when companies realized they had to streamline infrastructure and reduce their cost base to remain competitive. Whatever their popular name, these buzzwords fall into three broad categories:

1. *Activity value analysis.* Substantial near-term cost reductions tied directly to business productivity can be efficiently determined by teams of in-house staff that assess the value of tasks currently performed by line or staff personnel. *Activity-based accounting (ABA), activity value analysis (AVA), delayering, demassing, denominator management, downsizing,* and *rightsizing* are buzzwords associated with this category.

2. *Quality management.* The primary objectives of quality improvement programs are to eliminate rework, improve worker satisfaction, and increase customer loyalty. The link between quality and the current management focus on growth is strong. Buzzwords associated with quality, in addition to *TQM,* include

adhocracy, completeness, continuous improvement, centurions, and *empowerment.*

3. *Reengineering.* The most talked about business methodology and buzzword of the early '90s, *reengineering* goes beyond cost cutting and advocates fundamental changes in how a business operates. Other buzzwords in this category include *BPR (business process reengineering), change management, performance engineering*™, *restructuring,* and *reinventing.*

Question 4: Is the Buzzword Linked to Strategies for Growth?

Buzzwords related to growth strategies are being showcased in the business vocabulary of the mid-1990s. As management finishes wringing out excess costs and begins to explore how to increase market share in a slow growth macroeconomic environment, growth has become the new corporate watchword.

The buzzwords coming into the growth spotlight address a series of issues: customer retention, use of information technology, corporate transformation, and strategies for expansion.

1. *Customer retention.* A primary foundation for growth is, of course, acquiring attractive customers and keeping those who remain profitable. This strategy builds an ongoing annuity. Buzzwords associated with this topic include *customer franchise management, customer-centered organization, customer satisfaction, loyalty-based management, maxi-marketing,* and *zero defections.*

2. *Information technology.* Many management experts say that an information technology strategy can provide a key to gaining competitive advantage. They contend that a mature business can be revitalized and transformed into a new one by the way it captures, processes, and uses information to build a competitive product marketing and delivery strategy. Some buzzwords associated with the use of information technology are *channels marketing, fifth generation management, fourth generation management, hypercompetition, info-marketing, informate, informationalizing, mass customization,* and *segments of one.*

3. *Corporate transformation.* Building a competitive advantage requires that companies not only identify and cultivate their cur-

rent strengths but also cultivate a corporate culture that willingly transforms or reinvents the company on an ongoing basis. Those companies committed to transformation choose their own markets and the architecture for their organization rather than being driven by external forces. Buzzwords associated with the process include *breakpoint analysis, core competencies, discontinuous change, industry foresight, intellectual leadership, intelligent organization, intrapreneurship, knowledge-creating company, lateral thinking, learning organization, managerial frame, paradigm shift, s-curve analysis, six thinking hats, thunderbolt thinking,* and *upside-down thinking.*

4. *Strategies for expansion.* After a healthy company has determined how to keep its profitable customers, how best to service them, and, of course, what its unique competitive strengths are, it often discovers that growth requires walking the fine line of expansion versus cost containment. Growth may be limited by geography, the need for a complementary technology, or some other service that the company does not have within its four walls. Sustained growth may be tied into rethinking the corporate structure and becoming a *numerator manager.* Several options are usually available.

A company can either expand its staff and production line or affiliate with other organizations, including those that were previously considered direct competitors. Buzzwords that address the internal path for adjustable growth include *accordion management, flexible management, intrapreneuring,* and *the lean production model.*

Some buzzwords associated with external affiliations are *alliances, borderless/boundaryless companies, co-opetition, globalization, insiderization, just-in-time (JIT), PAL, partnerships,* and *co-ventures.*

Question 5: Does the Buzzword Represent a New Approach to Management?

For every buzzword that describes how to evaluate business operations and improve performance, it appears that five times as many address strategies for growth and ten times as many suggest new ways to manage a company and change its structure.

Why has the practice of management, as Peter Drucker called it, been the most fertile ground for buzzword growth? Pliable, abstract, and open to change, organizations provide abundant opportunities for management gurus to model social and economic microsystems and invent new names for them. Plus, managers under extreme pressure to improve profitability are willing to listen.

Buzzwords describing the new approaches to management fall into three categories:

1. *Models for the new organization.* How the new organization will fit together is an extremely popular topic in the academic and business press, generating many buzzwords. Whatever name is used for the new models, they share several characteristics: flexibility, an atmosphere of learning and entrepreneurial freedom, a process-oriented internal architecture. Among the buzzwords in this category are *federalism, horizontal corporation, human networking, lean production model, open-ended management, organizational architecture, shamrock organization, strategic architecture, team-driven, the virtual corporation,* and the *wired company.*

2. *Teams.* Teams may seem to be an apple-pie-and-motherhood concept that is easy to accept and easy to implement. But how to organize and foster teams based on empowered employee management is a core topic of much modern management theory. Among the key buzzwords associated with teams are *adhocracy, empowerment, high-performance workplace, participative management, self-leadership, self-managed work, team-driven organization,* and *teamnets.*

3. *Leadership.* As Charles Handy observes, in the new corporate enterprise taking shape the word *manager* is disappearing. Yet the concept of leadership is not abandoned. In fact, leadership has become closely tied to the issues of employee communication and empowerment. Management gurus repeatedly address the problem, and we find numerous leadership buzzwords including *postheroic leadership, return on management (ROM), servant leadership, stewardship, symbolic managers,* and *virtual leaders.*

Are Any Buzzwords MECE?

Actually, relatively few buzzwords fall into just one category and can be described as *MECE.* This acronym, used frequently by the consulting community, means that which is "mutually exclusive and collectively exhaustive" or, put more colloquially, "everything including the kitchen sink."

That connectivity between such categories as growth and the models for a new organization should not be surprising, given the linkage between areas such as quality and growth, profit analysis, and business expansion. Nonetheless, this set of five questions will provide an easy-to-follow path for businesspeople trying to make their way through the buzzword maze.

4

How to Create
a Buzzword

"The consultant concluded that it doesn't matter what it's called—it's what it does that's important."

—Christopher Lorenz, *The Financial Times*

Every executive who watches television has seen the computer-generated identity kits used in murder investigations. This software allows crime victims and witnesses to generate a picture of the accused assailant by mixing and matching a wide variety of facial shapes and features.

A walk through the business sections of bookstores across the United States and Europe can raise the suspicion that writers of management theory follow the same approach when choosing the titles for their books. Certain words appear again and again but in ever-different buzzword combinations.

Create a Buzzword

To test this theory, a do-it-yourself kit for creating a buzzword is easy to assemble. Everyone critical of the use of buzzwords should try their hand at this game of buzzword creation to gain both an appreciation of the difficulty of finding the right phrase and the sense of achievement that results from finding the word combination that best describes a management focus.

Would-be buzzword creators should start with a basic management idea that they wish to communicate and an equally firm idea of what they want users of the buzzword to do when they hear and use the word. The actual creation can be a simple, step-by-step process of selecting, at most, three words.

1. *Select a word that describes the "where."* Look for the direction or size that sets the scope for the buzzword, the theory, and the accompanying article or book. Words such as *global, local,* and *total* are frequent choices.
2. *Focus on the "how."* You will need to find the perfect word or phrase that describes the key lever that this emerging management theory will pull for the corporate world. Areas of management concern such as *customer, quality, service, technology, innovation,* and *product* are among the words of choice for this step of the creation process.
3. *Name "what" will be affected by this management theory.* Is it an institution? A business function? Organizational structure? Terms such as *management, marketing, partnering,* and *architecture* all appear frequently as buzzwords of choice.

Here is the raw material for a sample Buzzword Identi-Kit.

Buzzword Identi-Kit

Where	How	What
Beyond	Customer	Alliances
Co-	Franchise	Architecture
Global	Information	Competition
Hyper	Innovation	Corporation
Local	Process	Company
Maxi	Product	Management
On-demand	Quality	Marketing
Total	Value	Network
Upside-down	Service	Organization
Virtual	Support	Partnership

Some of the possible buzzword creations from this list include *hyper-innovation marketing, maxi-customer organization, global technology partnering,* and *upside-down service corporation.* The results of this "game" certainly sound as valid as many of the buzzword phrases being offered by management gurus today.

It would be a mistake, of course, to confuse the ability to create and trademark a buzzword with developing a meaningful approach or philosophy for management. At their best, buzzwords are the sound bytes that summarize a detailed and rich perspective on critical issues for managers to consider and act upon. Such buzzwords are like perfect seashells that can be held up to the ear again and again to echo the exact same sounds of a roaring ocean. At their worst, buzzwords are not backed up by substance and resemble pebbles tossed into a lake. They make a splash but then quickly disappear, never to be heard or seen again.

Buzzword Glossary

Most of the buzzwords described in the following glossary reflect serious management thought, although not all will endure beyond their fifteen minutes of fame. Don't hesitate to browse through these pages and cross-check entries. Add your own buzzwords, either as you find them or create them. The language of business has, indeed, changed, and the future belongs to those managers who can use it effectively and with imagination.

Part Two

A Buzzword Glossary

"The situation is unlikely to improve until teams share a new language for describing complexity."

—Peter Senge, *The Fifth Discipline*

Recently we received a lunchtime phone call from a young friend going through a series of intense interviews at a New York management consulting firm. All morning long she had been served up an alphabet soup of buzzwords—AVA, BPR, OES, TQM. As an outsider, she found the reliance on acronyms both disconcerting and amusing. "No one defined anything," she said. "Why did they think I would understand? Do you think they hand out dictionaries to new clients?"

Clearly our friend and her potential employers did not share a common language. In fact, we know a pension fund consultant who hands a dictionary of terms to his clients to ensure that both parties are going forward on the same track, at the same speed.

Corporate performance now demands a communications focus as well as a financial and monetary strategy for the wired organization. A new language of common definitions plus innovative ideas is needed to improve information flow and guarantee the ability to serve customers.

This Glossary puts the spotlight on over two hundred of the major buzzwords related to management strategy and organizational change. Each entry starts with a definition that places the buzzword in context of the corporate organization as well as the history of management theory. When known, the inventor or popularizer of the buzzword is credited. Oftentimes, however, the popularizer of a term is not the same person as its inventor.

Nearly all entries include a list of related terms, some of which are popular buzzwords that also appear in the Glossary. Many are synonyms; some are antonyms. Others are axioms in the same conceptual system. Then, to take the buzzword out of the classroom, this dictionary data is enriched by corporate examples illustrating the real-life impact of the management system communicated by the buzzword.

Finally, for those readers who desire to continue exploring the theories behind the buzzwords, we suggest heading for the nearest business bookstore or local library. As guidance we have included a suggested reading list for selected buzzwords. Many of these books and articles are single topic commentaries that cover a management theory intelligently and in depth. Recently a new genre of special interest magazines that cover business issues from the perspective of managing change in the information age has appeared, and those publications are also referenced.

accordian management   The ability to grow or shrink a workforce quickly at will by hiring or releasing temporary workers. Like an accordion, employment increases or drops based on the near-term requirements of a business. Job security is replaced by a highly flexible approach to staffing, which impacts both the blue- and white-collar ranks.

Related Terms   agile management, contingent workforce, flexible manufacturing, lean production model

Examples
- A *Time* magazine article provides the example of a Los Angeles woman who had been injured in an auto accident. When she asked the radiologist about a particular procedure she was undergoing, he replied: "Don't ask me; I'm only a temp."
- Lawsmiths is a firm in San Francisco that provides on-call lawyers, while Bank Temps in Denver provides temporary loan officers.
- IMCOR makes available senior executives who are expert at turnarounds. Says John Thompson who is the chairman, "Services like ours are going to flourish when businesses change so rapidly that it's in no one's interest to make commitments. Moving on to the next place you're needed is going to be the way it is."

Suggested Reading
Castro, Janice. "Disposable Workers." *Time,* March 29, 1993, p. 42.

activity value analysis (AVA)   A cost management strategy that builds a database to quantify the amount of time and personnel required to accomplish certain tasks and activities. By applying salary numbers to these items, management can gain valuable information about the dollar costs involved in achieving a task and determine the value of those activities to the company.

Virtually every consulting and accounting firm offers an AVA product whose primary focus is cost reduction. Although AVA has recently entered the management spotlight, one study traces its origins back to the 1920s.

AVA is particularly useful in examining the indirect overhead costs generated by staff areas, such as human resources and legal services, and separating out who performs what functions. As a result of an AVA, support services may continue to be insourced but under contractual arrangements competitive with purchasing them externally (outsourcing).

Using the data generated by an AVA, management can usually reduce operating expenses by a minimum of 15–20 percent. Effective use of employee-led teams to generate and evaluate the database can lead to permanent reductions in the cost base. AVA and related initiatives differ from reengineering in that they usually focus on marginal changes in approach rather than the more fundamental "clean blackboard" methodology promoted by reengineering.

Related Terms   activity-based accounting (ABA), activity-based costing (ABC), administrative value analysis, cost management, downsizing, organization analysis (OA), organization efficiency studies (OES), overhead value analysis (OVA), value costing

Examples
- After they see the cost accounting generated by AVA, many banks choose to redefine the role of the corporate relationship manager (RM) to concentrate on sales to new and existing customers. The banks then add a lower-paid staff member called a parabanker to handle customer service requests and administration. The added salary is more than compensated for by increased RM productivity.
- Transparent Container, a $21 million manufacturer of plastic containers based in Berkeley, Illinois, has said that by creating a pricing model that factored in possible actions and the resulting costs, it gained a broader understanding of corporate expenses at all levels. The information reportedly helped the company boost revenues and profit margins during the recession of the early 1990s.

Suggested Reading
Cooper, R., and R. S. Kaplan. "Measure Costs Right: Make the Right Decisions." *Harvard Business Review,* September–October 1988, pp. 96–103.

O'Guin, Michael. *A Complete Guide to Activity Based Accounting*. Englewood Cliffs, N.J.: Prentice-Hall, 1991.
Ostrenga, Michael R., Terence Ozan, Robert D. McIlhattan, and Marcus D. Harwood. *The Ernst & Young Guide to Total Cost Management*. New York: Wiley, 1992.

adhocracy   Buzzword that sets standards for team performance. Warren Bennis describes the formation of ad-hoc project teams that are "adaptive, problem-solving, temporary systems of diverse specialists linked together . . . in an organic flux."

Robert Waterman, who popularized the term which he says was created by Alvin Toffler, defines adhocracy as "any form of organization that cuts across normal bureaucratic lines to capture opportunities, solve problems, and gets results." Like many business buzzwords, adhocracy describes ways to circumvent the mind-numbing bureaucracy that characterizes many mature organizations and encourages individual creativity as part of a team commitment to corporate renewal.

Related Terms   collective leadership, empowerment, high-performance workplace, intelligent organization, knowledge-creating company, learning organization, teams, work groups

Examples
 • Waterman cites New York Life's 1986 design of a whole life policy as an example of adhocracy at its best. During two days of intense collaboration, an ad-hoc team composed of field agents, actuaries, designers, competition specialists, technicians, and service professionals from various parts of the country designed a new insurance product that increased New York Life's market share by two percentage points in two years.
 • The classic example of adhocracy, also cited by Waterman, may be the almost mythical story of Steve Jobs and his design team marching off to a separate building, hoisting the skull and crossbones flag in defiance of Apple Computer's bureaucracy, and designing the Macintosh.

Suggested Reading
Waterman, Robert H. Jr., *Adhocracy*. New York: Norton, 1992.

age of . . .   Term used by a number of management gurus to describe the current phase of change that business is going through:

Age of Chaos:	See Tom Peters, 1987. Chapter 2.
Age of Discontinuity:	See Discontinuous Change.

Age of Paradox: See Charles Handy, 1994.
Age of Unreason: See Charles Handy, 1989.

agile management   *See* accordian management, flexible management.

alliance   A popular description of the coalition strategies for swapping skills as well as sharing values and the costs generated when companies seek to expand their markets. Corporations that form alliances are willing to collaborate with competitors or suppliers of complementary products and services to avoid crippling capital investments and gain local market insight or core competencies.

McKinsey consultants Joel Bleeke and David Ernst see the alliance—similar to the *entente* of global politics—as the prototype for the flexible, amoebalike corporate structure of the future. They predict that the product-oriented sales culture of today's hierarchical organization will not survive in the emerging global marketplace that will demand quick and customized product development.

Gary Hamel and C. K. Prahalad suggest that in the future competition will be as much a battle between competing alliances as between individual firms. Companies that succeed in alliances will make a commitment to communicate, share control through negotiated compromise, and bridge cultural hurdles as well as geographic boundaries.

Alliances can usually be divided into four categories according to Neil Buckley who writes for *The Financial Times:*

1. *Cooperative buying.* These groups increase the purchasing power that partners have with manufacturers.
2. *Skills-based.* In this alliance, partners have skills or knowledge of a market that each other lacks.
3. *Development-based.* These alliances are usually built around development of a project such as entry into a new market or a product.
4. *Multifunctional.* These alliances encompass elements of each of the three types described above.

Alliances are forged because of the complementary benefits each partner brings to the other. Although a partner's ability to become fully functional in a particular geographic area or market may then be limited, alliances are usually pursued precisely because a member has chosen not to pursue full participation.

Related Terms   co-ventures, crossborder mergers and acquisitions, globalization, joint ventures, *keiretsu* (group companies), PALs (pooling, allying, linking companies), partnering, partnerships

Examples   Examples of alliances abound among Japanese, European, and American companies in the automotive, pharmaceutical, semiconductor, nuclear power, and recently, in financial services, publishing, retailing, telecommunications, and software industries.

- In 1994, GE Capital began planning a move into the Japanese consumer credit market by purchasing Mineba, the credit and consumer finance subsidiary of a Japanese bearings company.
- AT&T Corp. has announced a multimedia alliance with Silicon Graphics Inc. to sell that company's computerized video transmission gear. The agreement helps AT&T add to its already extensive line of equipment for the information superhighway and gives Silicon Graphics an entry into that market.
- Paramount Communications Inc.'s publishing arm and Davidson & Associates, a computer software firm, announced a development-based alliance in 1994 to produce a range of multimedia products using Paramount's library of titles. Paramount executives said that they see such alliances as the "wave of the future," putting money into product development instead of stock.
- Sainsbury, the United Kingdom's largest grocery retailer, recently announced a formal partnership to be called SEDD with three other European retailers—Esselunga of Italy, Delhaize of Belgium, and Dockoder France. Under the multifunctional alliance, the four groups will share expertise and cooperate in buying and marketing.

Suggested Reading

Bleeke, Joel, and David Ernst, eds. *Collaborating to Compete: Using Strategic Alliances and Acquisitions in the Global Marketplace.* New York: Wiley, 1993.

Buckley, Neil. "Baked Beans Across Europe." *The Financial Times,* April 14, 1994, p. 9.

Hamel, Gary, and C. K. Prahalad. *Competing for the Future: Breakthrough Strategies for Seizing Control of Your Industry and Creating the Markets of Tomorrow.* Boston: Harvard Business School Press, 1994.

Kanter, Rosabeth Moss. "Collaborative Advantage: The Age of Alliances." *Harvard Business Review,* July–August 1994, pp. 96–108.

Ohmae, Kenichi, *Triad Power: The Coming Shape of Global Competition.* New York: Free Press, 1985.

AVA *See* activity value analysis.

balanced scorecard Developed by Robert Kaplan and David Norton, a measurement system that links corporate strategy with four key scores or measures for judging performance: financial, customer-related, internal business, and growth. Financial measures include return on capital, cash flow, profitability, and the quality of earnings. Customer-related measures include satisfaction and market share analysis; internal business measures include quantification of re-works, bid success rates, and safety performance. Finally, growth-related measures focus on the percent of revenues from new products or services, revenue per employee, and even the number of suggestions submitted by employees.

The value of the balanced scorecard derives from the link between these measurements and the integrated corporate values that this approach emphasizes. To create a true measure a company must decide what its critical success factors are in terms of its shareholders, customers, internal management processes, and growth opportunities before calculating the specific measures for each of the four areas. How well actual performance measures up against the success factors can then prompt decisions on lines of business and products, such as where to conduct benchmark surveys and other analysis.

Related Terms   benchmarking, best practices, critical success factors, MBO (management by objective)

Example
- In mid-1994, Goodyear Tire & Rubber Co. announced a four-year plan to increase operating profit margins through productivity and to boost sales through new products. At analysts' meetings held in New York, the company's chairman described the plan that included the following financial measures: a cut in expenses, an increase in capital expenditure, a reduced debt-to-equity ratio, and a new dividend policy.

Suggested Reading
Kaplan, Robert S., and David P. Norton. "Putting the Balanced Score-card to Work." *Harvard Business Review,* vol. 71, no. 5, September–October 1993, pp. 134–147.

benchmarking   A practice that involves evaluating and comparing how key functions and processes are performed both within one's company and at other companies, only some of whom need to be direct competitors. When used with best practices, benchmarking can provide a yardstick for growth.

External benchmarking identifies best practices that can be adapted to a company's own organization. A continuous process of internal benchmarking allows a company to capture and communicate the best practices of a company's own salespeople or manufacturing units that are outstanding performers. External comparisons involving companies in similar industries provide a measure for the corporate enterprise that wants to stay ahead of the competition.

Virtually all companies can take advantage of benchmarking and, by applying internal and external best practices, build a yardstick for growth. Benchmarking, however, may also become a circular trap or create a glass ceiling that limits the creativity of a company's management and staff.

Related Terms   balanced scorecard, best practices, continuous improvement, performance improvement, quality practices, reverse engineering

Examples

- McDonald's, L.L. Bean, Neiman Marcus, the Ritz Carlton Hotels, and Wachovia Bank provide benchmark examples of best practices in customer service.
- A 1994 benchmark survey by *The Financial Times* and Price Waterhouse identified Deutsche Bank as the financial services company most respected by Europe's senior executives.
- UPS, American Airlines, and American Express are commonly cited for their use of information technology to create competitive advantage.

Suggested Reading

Spendolini, Michael J. *The Benchmarking Book.* New York: AMACOM, 1992.

Taylor, Paul. "Benchmark is set by clear winners in product groups." *The Financial Times,* June 27, 1994, p. 9.

Watson, Gregory H. *Strategic Benchmarking: How to Rate Your Company's Performance Against the World's Best.* New York: Wiley, 1993.

best practices   Old standard consulting term now a full-fledged buzzword frequently invoked by corporate executives who seek to emulate the best. Best practices are exactly what the term implies—the highest standards of performance in specifically defined categories such as customer service, sales, marketing, and product innovation.

Related Terms   benchmarking, reverse engineering

Examples

- Nucor Steel and Asea Brown Boveri (ABB) are frequently cited as best practices examples for their management of overhead and employee empowerment.
- AT&T and Xerox provide examples of best practices for quality and customer service.
- Malcolm Baldrige Award winners provide examples of best practices in customer service.
- Arthur Andersen promotes its Global Best Practices proprietary knowledge base as a tool that companies can use for comparing their operating practices to the best in the world.

Suggested Reading
> Bogan, Christopher, and M. English. *Benchmarking for Best Practices.* New York: McGraw-Hill, Inc., 1994.
> Watson, Gregory H. *The Benchmarking Workbook: Adapting Best Practices for Performance Improvement.* Cambridge, Mass.: Productivity Press, 1992.

beyond loyalty   A Tom Peters signature phrase for the new mind-set whereby employees look to their own best interests even while serving the needs of their corporate employer.

big three model of change   A Rosabeth Moss Kanter signature phrase for an organizational model that explores how corporations operate and manage the process when internal and external forces precipitate change. *See* change management.

boss management   Management system that focuses on production quotas and speed of production based on the stimulus response theory of human behavior. The system, as defined by William Glasser, covers four steps:

Step 1	Management sets a task.
Step 2	Workers are told rather than shown how to complete the task.
Step 3	The "boss" or a designated management supervisor inspects the work.
Step 4	Failure to produce quality work is met with coercion or punishment.

This system leads to an adversarial workplace of management versus the workers. Boss management is generally seen as the opposite of lead management, a characteristic of quality management systems such as those advocated by W. Edwards Deming.

Related Terms   command and control management, MBD (management by decree)

Examples
- Until fairly recently, automobile assembly lines have been run by boss management techniques. A strict schedule of production quotas prevailed, and workers had no discretion to halt production even if they detected flaws.

Suggested Reading
> Glasser, William. *The Control Theory Manager: Combining the Control Theory of William Glasser With the Wisdom of W. Edwards Deming to*

Explain Both What Quality Is and What Lead Managers Do to Achieve It. New York: HarperCollins, 1994.

borderless organization   *See* alliance, federalism, globalization, virtual corporation.

bottom-up participation   *See* empowerment, followership, middle-up-down management.

boundaryless organization   *See* federalism, globalization, virtual corporation.

BPR (business process reengineering)   Reorganizing a company around essential business processes, such as sales and customer service, flattening the corporate hierarchy, and staffing the organization with multidisciplinary teams of experts.

One key way that reengineering around processes is distinctive from traditional vertical management is that customer priorities drive decisions about the way work is done.

Related Terms   business process improvement, business process management, process redesign, customer franchise management, performance reengineering™, reengineering

Examples
- At Hallmark cards, teams of writers, editors, artists, and production specialists work closely with sales, distribution, graphic arts, and manufacturing to develop products. As a result of this team focus, the production time for new versions of Shoebox greeting cards was cut from nine to three months.
- Sun Life Assurance of Canada identified the business process of serving upscale buyers quickly and effectively as the linchpin of its sales effort. Eight-person teams now work together to expedite all requests, a system which avoids the need to switch customer calls from one specialist to another.

Suggested Reading
Grant, Linda. "New Jewel in the Crown." *U.S. News & World Report,* February 28, 1994.
Johansson, Henry J., Patrick McHugh, A. John Pendlebury, William A. Wheeler III. *Business Process Reengineering: BreakPoint Strategies for Market Dominance.* New York: Wiley, 1993.

breakpoint   An innovation or radical departure from marketplace expectations that creates unrealized opportunities to seize market share by choosing customer and management expectations. An essential supplement to bean-counting restructuring exercises, breakpoint strategies are part of the renewal or transformation process that can force a new way of thinking and catapult a company into a leadership position.

Related Terms benchmarking, business process reengineering (BPR), charge management, completeness, discontinuous change, gazelle, lateral thinking, outside-the-box thinking, paradigm shift, s-curve analysis, thunderbolt thinking

Examples
- Philips, the world's third largest consumer electronics company, based in The Netherlands, slashed 70,000 jobs and cut money-losing businesses, bringing the company from a loss position in 1992 to over a billion dollar profit in 1993. To remain competitive with other global electronics powerhouses, however, the company realized that cost restructuring alone was not the solution; it needed to turn core research into hit products that seize market dominance. In other words, Philips realized that it needed to find a breakpoint. To change the inward-looking corporate culture, senior executives have been shifted, and an acquisition strategy was undertaken in 1994. Three new technologies—digital compact cassettes, compact disc interactive (CD-i) technology, and active-matrix flat-panel displays—have been launched.
- Paul Strebel cites both Drexel Burnham Lambert's promotion of the junk bond market and that market's collapse as breakpoints.
- The number of companies that have failed to take advantage of possible breakpoint innovations in technology is, perhaps, larger than those that have. For example, neither Digital nor IBM wholeheartedly pursued the emergence of personal computers, underrating the influence that the PC would have on their mainframe businesses.

Suggested Reading
Edmondson, Gail, Neil Gross, Patrick Oster. "Philips Needs Laser Speed." *Business Week,* June 6, 1994, pp. 46–47.

Johansson, Henry J., Patrick McHugh, A. John Pendlebury, William A. Wheeler III. *Business Process Reengineering: BreakPoint Strategies for Market Dominance.* New York: Wiley, 1993.

Strebel, Paul. *Breakpoints: How Managers Exploit Radical Business Change.* Boston: Harvard Business School Press, 1992.

Utterback, James. *Mastering the Dynamics of Innovation: How Companies Can Seize Opportunities in the Face of Technological Change.* Boston: Harvard Business School Press, 1994.

buckyborgs A Tom Peters term for clusters of fifty- to sixty-person business units that form teams within the new organization structures taking shape. *See* teams, virtual corporation.

bunsha   Management philosophy of breaking up a company into ever smaller business units centered around a product or service. Following World War II, Kuniyasu Sakai and Hiroshi Sekiyama started a business in Japan which has since become very profitable and is now known as the Bunsha Group of companies. Rather than build an industrial giant such as Sony or Mitsubishi, however, Sakai and Sekiyama pursued another path to success—company division.

Sakai and Sekiyama believe that as companies grow larger the number of employees who feel directly responsible for the organization's success grows smaller and smaller. Dividing a company reverses that trend, reenergizing the workforce and making it clear that individual employees and their needs are the primary concern of management.

When a company becomes stable and appears to be moving on a steady course, Sakai and Sekiyama see this as the optimum time to divide, avoiding the complacency and bureaucracy of mature firms and gaining the energy and drive to succeed that is characteristic of young companies. Employees discover their potential for creativity and can reach new levels of productivity.

This bunsha strategy of decentralizing and breaking up the corporate entity into groups of smaller companies has placed both executives in demand as consultants to Japanese companies. Mr. Sakai has also lectured on the concept worldwide.

Related Terms   breakpoint strategy, empowerment, federalism, *keiretsu*, no excuses management, s-curve analysis, spinouts

Examples

- Sakai and Sekiyama put their theory into action as they built the Bunsha Group consisting of dozens of highly successful companies. Starting with an industrial painting company, the two expanded by dividing their company into related firms such as a machine shop and a producer of electronics components.

Suggested Reading

Sakai, Kuniyasu, and Hiroshi Sekiyama, as told to David Russell. *Bunsha: Improving Your Business Through Company Division*. New York: Intercultural Group, 1985.

centurion   *See* completeness.

change management   The process of reinventing or restructuring a corporation's culture, its business strategy, and/or organization structure, so called because of the radical break from past business practices that most new change management theories, such as reengineering or breakpoint analysis, advocate.

The ability to manage rapid change, anticipate opportunities in a dynamic marketplace, and develop the appropriate core competencies has become a measure of success for excellent companies of the mid-1990s.

Related Terms   big three model of change, breakpoint, BPR, change masters, core competencies, corporate transformation, opportunity horizon, reengineering

Examples

- In its recent survey of European companies, The Conference Board reported that more than half said that they began their current round of change management in 1989. Fifty percent of the companies said they had changed their leadership and culture; 40 percent had changed their use of information technology; and more than half had overhauled their business strategies, organization structure, and composition of the workforce.
- Gerald Ross, cofounder of Change Lab International, a Greenwich, Connecticut consulting firm, is a change management expert whose clients include Bristol-Meyers Squibb. He believes that the new molecular organization produced by change management will be built around markets, not products or functions.

Suggested Reading

Byrne, John. "Management's New Gurus." *Business Week*, August 31, 1992, pp. 44–52.

"Change brings results." *The Financial Times*, June 22, 1994.

Change Management: An Overview of Current Initiatives. Report No. 1068-94-RR, The Conference Board Europe, Avenue Louise 207, Box 5, B-1050 Brussels, Belgium.

Heifetz, Michael L. *Leading Change, Overcoming Chaos: A Seven Stage Process for Making Change Succeed in Your Organization.* Berkeley, Calif.: Ten Speed Press, 1993.

Kanter, Rosabeth Moss, Barry A. Stein, and Todd D. Jick. *The Challenge of Organizational Change: How Companies Experience It and Leaders Guide It.* New York: Free Press, 1992.

Kanter, Rosabeth Moss. *The Change Masters: Corporate Entrepreneurs at Work.* New York: Simon & Schuster, 1983.

Peters, Tom. *The Tom Peters Seminar: Crazy Times Call for Crazy Organizations.* New York: Vintage, 1994.

channels management   The focused use of sales distribution channels to achieve strategic goals—a way to leverage growth.

The use of specific sales channels—the methods of marketing and distributing a product—already accounts for a large portion of the value added in many service industries and will increasingly determine success in acquiring and retaining customers as well as generating profitable growth.

The proliferation of sales channels ranging from "800" numbers to overnight mail and the Internet has been driven by the emergence of digital technology and by the opportunities for mass customization. The "new" information-age customer created by this multichannel environment has already developed increased expectations for quality, variety, and ease of access.

Related Terms   customer franchise management, growth, mass customization, multichannel product delivery systems

Examples
- The growth in sales channels has been noteworthy in the mutual funds industry where the importance of financial advisors and retail brokers is diminishing while the influence of direct marketing and access through financial institutions such as mutual fund companies and banks is increasing. The number of alternative distribution channels such as insurance agents, interactive ATMs, and online services is also quickly growing.
- Home-shopping channels have brought the shopping mall to television.

Suggested Reading
Atkins, Robert G., and N. Andrew Cohen. "Sales Channel Management: The Power of Innovation at the Point of Customer Contact." *Mercer Management Journal*, no. 2, 1994, pp. 9–27.

co-branding   The cosponsoring of a customer product or financial service, such as a credit card, by two independent corporate enterprises trying to gain entry into a market that neither feels it can profitably enter alone. *See* alliance, co-opetition, co-venture, partnering/partnerships.

collective leadership   *See* adhocracy, empowerment, team, work group.

collective learning   *See* core competencies.

competitive advantage   Michael Porter's signature phrase for discussing competitive strategy. *See* industry foresight, opportunity.

competitive innovation   Signature phrase of Gary Hamel and C. K. Prahalad. *See* industry foresight, opportunity.

competitive strategy   *See* industry foresight, opportunity.

completeness   Success in attaining quality in all parts of the corporate organization (Crosby, 1994). Philip Crosby argues that if attention is paid to the whole corporate picture, from the quality of products and customer service to the initiative of employees and, of course, the bottom line, the result will be a state of completeness.

Crosby's philosophy of completeness is derived from the guiding principles of W. Edwards Deming's quality management philosophy: that how well processes work together is the most important facet of any organizational theory.

Crosby states that the purpose of completeness as he envisions it is to avoid problems and guarantee success of three key constituencies: employees, suppliers, and customers. Providing the leadership for this twenty-first century movement will be a group of individuals whom Crosby names Centurions, borrowing a title given to Roman officers who led the legions, to distinguish them from nineteenth and twentieth century leaders. These individuals will be characterized by their ability to build human and computer networks and their willingness to communicate and share information in the drive to attain completeness.

Related Terms   centurion, TQM

Examples
- Netherlands-based electronics giant Philips launched a renewal project in the early 1990s to promote new ways of thinking and named it Operation Centurion.
- Crosby takes the concept of completeness out of the corporate boardroom and into society, where he envisions that a bottom-up socialism will occur where the people not only take on the task of making their business and personal life better but also limit the role of government to essential functions that provide infrastructure such as delivering the mail.

Suggested Reading
Crosby, Philip. *Completeness: Quality for the 21st Century.* New York: Penguin Books, 1994.

complexification   Popularized by John Casti to discuss the science of surprise, which addresses the question of why our universe, including business operations, seems so paradoxical. To explain complexification, Casti, a mathematician, explores "the rules of reality, their form, nature, and idiosyncracies." His treatise is particularly applicable to modern business management issues. It recognizes the impossibility of predicting the total range of chance factors and how their interaction may affect the outcome of an event in a complex, as opposed to a basic, system.

Many business theorists, notably Charles Handy and Tom Peters, have also taken a step outside-the-box to address the paradoxical issues and chaos both arising from and causing the changes in corporate, government, and social life that began in the early 1990s.

Related Terms   age of discontinuity, age of paradox, chaos theory, science of surprise

Examples

- Maverick economist Brian Arthur of the Santa Fe Institute has argued that the real economy does not work at all the way the traditional models of economics developed by Adam Smith say it should. It is much more complex. Rather than believe, for example, that where demand exists for goods, prices will reflect the level where supply equals demand, Arthur argues that price is impacted by positive feedback which cannot be predicted.

  Using Arthur's theory as an example of complexification, in his book Casti cites the way VHS cassette recorders won market dominance from Beta cassettes. In their recent book on competitive strategy Hamel and Prahalad also cite the same product competition as an example of the complex factors influencing the outcome of industry competition.

  Both versions of the cassette recorder were introduced at relatively the same time and initially had the same market share. Although Beta is often described as a superior technology, VHS has taken over the entire market. Chance factors such as "luck" and marketing savvy affected the outcome of this market fight rather than logical economic equilibrium.

Suggested Reading

Casti, John. *Complexification*. New York: HarperCollins, 1994.

Hamel, Gary, and C. K. Prahalad. *Competing for the Future: Breakthrough Strategies for Seizing Control of Your Industry and Creating the Markets of Tomorrow*. Boston: Harvard Business School Press, 1994.

Handy, Charles. *The Age of Paradox*. Boston: Harvard Business School Press, 1994.

Peters, Tom. *Thriving on Chaos: Handbook for a Management Revolution*. New York: Knopf, 1987.

contingency workforce   Individuals hired by companies to work on short-range projects or to cover unexpected demands that cannot be met by a permanent core group of employees. One out of five Americans is now a member of the contingency workforce.

  By tapping into this floating employment reservoir, which is also called the contingent workforce, corporations gain access to top talent, keep benefit costs from mushrooming, and still meet seasonal or project demands requiring additional staff.

  In corporations impacted by reductions in workforce that resulted from downsizing strategies, the demand for interim professionals has created a new class of professional temporaries vastly differently in education and professional experience from clerical temporary workers. These individuals may freelance from their home or work as on-site professionals. Corporations often purchase their services through an agency that specializes in placing part-time, temporary, or full-time professional workers.

Related Terms accordian management, contingent workforce, execu-temps, freelancers, head-renters (temporary placement agencies), independent contractors, interim executives, just-in-time employees, lean production model, shamrock organization, temporary executives, throwaway executives

Examples
- The contingency workforce includes members of all professions. They range from a Yale-educated lawyer who decided she wanted the flexibility to pursue a career in training and education when her first child was born to computer programmers who avoid corporate politics and thrive on the challenge of developing new software.
- The new workforce also includes laid-off workers who are having difficulty finding full-time, permanent employment and those who want the opportunity to explore different career paths. Some workers, including public relations professionals and laboratory technicians, make a career of temporary work, thriving on the challenge of new assignments and avoiding the boredom of repetitive work.
- In an essay for *Forbes,* Casper W. Weinberger argued that allowing unions to represent "contingent" or temporary workers and extending the benefits enjoyed by permanent workers would increase consumer costs.
- Management consulting is a profession based on a company's need for a project-based contingent workforce.

Suggested Reading
Executive Recruiter News, an industry trade journal.
Fierman, Jaclyn. "The Contingency Work Force." *Fortune,* January 24, 1994, vol. 129, no. 2, pp. 30–36.
Handy, Charles. *The Age of Paradox.* Boston: Harvard Business School Press, 1994.
Nollen, Stanley. *Work Schedules in Practice: Managing Time in a Changing Society.* New York: Van Nostrand Reinhold, 1982.

continuous improvement English expression for the Japanese quality management term *kaizen,* which describes ongoing or continuous improvement in the production process. It is led by management but can be successful only with the cooperation and input of the company's workforce. This continuous process can addresses specific ways to improve the organization, such as the physical layout of the production line, scheduling, and supply systems, or customer service or new products. A basic tenet of the system is to challenge employee perceptions of existing procedures continuously rather than command blind adherence to them.

Related Terms   empowerment, control theory, *kaizen,* knowledge-creating company, market-driven management, TQM

Examples
- At the General Motors Opel plant in Eisenbach, East Germany, workers who follow the *kaizen* philosophy came up with the suggestion to redesign supply boxes to tilt forward as they become empty, thus saving time reaching for parts.
- At a small car accessory factory in Bedfordshire, England, introduction of *kaizen* methodology resulted in a redesign of the shop floor, increasing productivity on some product lines up to 30 percent.

Suggested Reading
> Bowles, Jerry, and Joshua Hammond. *Beyond Quality: How 50 Winning Companies Use Continuous Improvement.* New York: Putnam, 1991.
> Imai, Masaaki. *Kaizen (Ky'zen)—The Key to Japan's Competitive Success.* New York: McGraw Hill, 1986.
> Rehfeld, John E. *Alchemy of a Leader: Combining Western and Japanese Management Skills to Transform Your Company.* New York: Wiley, 1994.

continuous innovation   *See* knowledge-creating company.

control theory   Described as a theory of intrinsic motivation by William Glasser. Around since the 1980s, control theory is a further development of the quality management theory of W. Edwards Deming. It promotes a management system where managers first learn to discern what quality is and how to teach it to the workforce. Then, they listen to all suggestions for improvement and lead the workforce, convincing them that "it is to their benefit to settle for nothing less than quality."

Related Terms   continuous improvement, lead management, TQM

Examples
- The Saturn automobile assembly line provides an example of control theory in practice. Workers on the Saturn line are responsible for bringing production to a halt if they detect any problem with

the car being assembled, whether or not the fault relates to their immediate task. Saturn provides straps similar to the emergency cords on trains that give each worker the control to stop the line. As a result, Saturn cars have gained an excellent reputation for quality.

Suggested Reading

Glasser, William. *The Control Theory Manager: Combining the Control Theory of William Glasser With the Wisdom of W. Edwards Deming to Explain Both What Quality Is and What Lead Managers Do to Achieve It.* New York: HarperCollins, 1994.

co-opetition New buzzword for a concept that has received attention for several years, that is, working with competitors to take advantage of their manufacturing, distribution, or other capabilities. Recognizing the need to cooperate and compete at the same time, some companies are beginning to view competitors who manufacture and sell complementary goods/services as potential joint venture partners.

Related Terms alliance, co-branding, co-venturing, PAL (pool resources; ally to exploit an opportunity; link systems), partnering, virtual corporation

Examples

- AT&T competes with major commercial banks in the credit card business while it also works with them to develop a payment system using debt cards. AT&T, through its NCR subsidiary, is also a major supplier of hardware and software to the banking industry.
- France Telecom has joined with a number of other telecommunications companies to invest in General Magic Inc., a California company that is setting the standard for wireless personal communications by developing "electronic navigator" software that scans complex computer networks for users.
- Delta Consulting, a first-tier firm in the senior management advisory market, works alone but also with McKinsey & Co., a direct competitor, on management restructuring projects as well as with fellow competitors Monitor, Markon, and Coopers & Lybrand on strategy and operations projects.

Suggested Reading

Kanter, Rosabeth Moss. *When Giants Learn to Dance.* New York: Simon & Schuster, 1989.

Lipnack, Jessica, and Jeffrey Stamps. *The TeamNet Factor.* Essex Junction, Vt.: Oliver Wight, 1993.

core competencies Describes the traditional strengths or skills and knowledge that give a company its intrinsic competitive advantage in the marketplace. C. K. Prahalad, a professor of corporate strategy and international business at the University of Michigan, and Gary Hamel, a lecturer in business policy and management at the London Business School, have adapted the term core competencies from the human resources lexicon.

When successful corporations are described using this management construct, they are portrayed as a portfolio of potentially reinforcing competencies that are embodied in human skills, are not transferable, and cannot be easily imitated.

Core competencies are not the same as brand dominance or product market share; they are, instead, the often-unrecognized skills—the collective learning—that make these end products possible.

Hamel and Prahalad advocate that companies define their core competencies in terms of their core technology and core products. They predict that those companies that build market power in tomorrow's fast-moving markets will concentrate on the triumvirate of core competencies, core products, and end products rather than end product market share or even price performance between finished products.

Companies need to assess their current core competencies and those required for future success and, then, develop a road map to achieve them.

Related Terms   collective learning, complementary capabilities, core products, declutter, end products, out-of-the-mainstream capabilities, strategic architecture

Examples
- To cut its bloated operating costs, Honeywell began the effort to refocus on its core competencies as a manufacturer and installer of controls in 1986. The Minneapolis company sold its computer business, spun off defense operations, and cut the workforce by 30 percent. Honeywell has now returned to its core businesses. The company has found creativity in expanding its end product line to include security systems for homes, process monitors for paper mills, smoke detection devices, and navigation systems.
- R. R. Donnelley repositioned its core competency of industrial printing while cutting costs and redefining both its core products and end products. The company now packages and transmits information not only by putting ink on paper but also through a direct mail operation and satellite, facsimile, and compact disc transmission.
- Chrysler is cited as a company that allowed one of its core compe-

tencies, engine technology, to wither. During the 1980s, the company outsourced production of automobile engines to Mitsubishi and Hyundai, and its "competency" or skill in engine design faded.

- To concentrate on its core competencies with financial services, the U.S. money center bank Citicorp has sold a number of nonstrategic services, including I/B/E/S Inc., a supplier of corporate earnings estimates.

Suggested Reading

> Henkoff, Ronald. "Getting Beyond Downsizing." *Fortune,* vol. 129, no. 1, January 10, 1994, pp. 58–64.
>
> Prahalad, C. K., and Gary Hamel. "The Core Competence of the Corporation." *Harvard Business Review,* vol. 68, no. 3, May–June 1990, pp. 79–91.

core products   Key components or modules within end products. Gary Hamel and C. K. Prahalad challenge traditional views of industrial competition by shifting the perspective to value analysis. Rather than focus on the market share in finished, or as they name them, end products, Hamel and Prahalad suggest that manufacturers should understand that success depends on their share of the market in core products.

> In most industries, core product modules are investment intensive, require large-scale development, and can be sold to companies that require the item but wish to dedicate resources to their own core products. In many cases, suppliers of these core products may be competitors.

Related Terms   co-opetition, core business, core competence, core franchise, core profitability, core technology, end products, intercluster competition, open clusters, virtual integration

Examples

- Three-fourths of the world's fax machines, an estimated 20 million pieces sold under multiple brand names, communicate with a modem made by Rockwell, giving the company a leadership position in this core electronics product.
- Compact disc mechanisms are a core product for Sony, which has over a 60 percent world market share and sells aggressively to Japanese and Asian competitors who make rival audio components.
- Service-related examples also exist. In its April 1994 assessment of Chemical Banking Corporation's ratings, Moody's Investor Service cited the bank's aggressive pursuit of its core franchises.

Suggested Reading

> Prahalad C. K., and Gary Hamel. "The Core Competence of the Corporation." *Harvard Business Review,* vol. 68, no. 3, May–June 1990, pp. 79–91.

corporate anorexia   Description by Professor Gary Hamel of the London Business School for corporations that cut costs and staff without redesigning jobs or revitalizing the corporate spirit.

These downsized companies often find that the most talented and mobile people find other jobs, leaving a dispirited and overworked core workforce whose productivity may decline and whose attention to customer service is low.

Related Terms   delayering, demassing, downsizing, rightsizing

Examples
- At Nynex, the New York area telephone company where 20,000 jobs were cut between 1984 and 1994 and a further 20 percent reduction is planned during 1994–1997, service complaints have risen. In regulatory hearings, New York State's attorney general argued that Nynex provides the poorest service among the 40 telephone companies serving New York.

Suggested Reading
Rose, Frederick. "Job-Cutting Medicine Fails to Remedy Productivity Ills at Many Companies." *The Wall Street Journal,* June 7, 1994, p. A2.
Tomasko, Robert. *Downsizing: Reshaping the Corporation for the Future.* New York: AMACOM, 1990.

corporate decomposition   Signature phrase of David Nadler that describes the result of rethinking the traditional structure of an organization. Rigid, vertical bureaucracy will give way to an autonomous, high-performance workforce of self-empowered employees.

corporate genetics   Gary Hamel and C. K. Prahalad's term for the set of biases and assumptions a company's management and employees hold about an industry—including the competition, profitability, customers, the technological applications, shareholder values, and employee interests and motivations. *See* managerial frame.

corporate graffiti   New business terms that pop up in a seemingly random and occasionally subversive fashion similar to the scrawls found on subway walls. Many business buzzwords make their first appearance as corporate graffiti. Corporate graffiti may appear in memorandums or presentations by management consultants or by specialized business units to describe business phenomena. *See* Chapter 1: What's in a Word?

corporate transformation   Definition of this phenomenon varies from management guru to management guru. Each definition, however, shares a vision of a corporation that actively recognizes the need to reinvent or restructure a part or all of its corporate structure to outpace changes in the marketplace or technology. Such an ideal company takes charge of its own destiny both by reviewing its goals and expectations and by taking the actions necessary to achieve them.

One framework for analyzing corporate transformation has been developed by Barbara Blumenthal, an adjunct professor of management at Temple University, and Philippe Haspeslagh, professor of business policy, Corporate Renewal Initiative, at INSEAD. Blumenthal and Haspeslagh offer criteria for three types of corporate transformation that can help companies remain competitive in a dynamic marketplace: improvements in operations, strategic transformation, and corporate self-renewal. Their definition of corporate transformation highlights behavior and makes a distinction between transformation and other changes, such as restructuring, that may result from a merger.

The prerequisite for success in each instance, according to Blumenthal and Haspeslagh, is management's ongoing commitment and effort to overcome employee resistance to change.

Related Terms   age of chaos, age of discontinuity, age of paradox, age of unreason, breakpoint, change management, discontinuous change, learning organization, reengineering, reinventing, renewal factor, s-curve analysis, transformation agenda, transformational leader, turnaround

Examples

- Blumenthal and Haspeslagh cite British Airways' decision to differentiate itself by focusing on marketing and customer service as an example of a corporate transformation. Each employee, including senior management, is required to take a series of Customer First seminars to reinforce the corporate dedication to customer service.
- General Motors' Saturn car is an example of corporate transformation from concept and manufacturing to marketing, sales, and follow-up service.

Suggested Reading

Beer, M., R. Eisenstat, and B. Spector. "Why Change Programs Don't Produce Change." *Harvard Business Review,* November–December 1990, pp. 158–166.

Blumenthal, Barbara, and Philippe C. Haspeslagh. "Toward a Definition of Corporate Transformation." *Sloan Management Review,* Spring 1994, pp. 101–106.

Davis, Stan, and Bill Davidson. *2020 Vision: Transform Your Business Today to Succeed in Tomorrow's Economy.* New York: Simon & Schuster, 1991.

Drucker, Peter, "A Turnaround Primer." *The Wall Street Journal*, February 2, 1993, p. A14.

Semler, Ricardo. *Maverick: The Success Story Behind the World's Most Unusual Workplace*. New York: Warner Books, 1993.

corporateur   An entrepreneur who operates within the corporate structure pursuing innovative projects. *See* corporate venturing, intrapreneuring.

corporate venturing   An innovative research and development strategy that encourages internal diversification under high-level senior management sponsorship.

     Successful corporate ventures are usually housed inside the mainstream business and are subject to performance expectations within a set time frame. These ventures are also usually kept largely free from planning and control systems that can strangle a new operation under the workload of paper and the constraints of risk management compliance. Critics debate whether these intercompany ventures can actually provide a return quickly enough to merit the extra investment of management time and R&D funds. Corporate cultures that foster this type of innovation demand that management be willing to accept and learn from failures as well as successes.

Related Terms   intrapreneurship, corporate entrepreneurs, corporateur, learning organization

Examples

- Hewlett-Packard and 3M are two creative companies that have built a corporate culture that encourages entrepreneurial ventures and allows new projects to grow, become profitable, or fail on their own merits rather than collapsing under excessive administrative restrictions before they reach critical capacity.

Suggested Reading

Block, Zena, and Ian C. MacMillan. *Corporate Venturing: Creating New Businesses Within the Firm*. Boston: Harvard Business School Press, 1993.

cost management   Expense and overhead control. The basic disciplines of cost management are being viewed by many companies with renewed respect as a way to build competitive advantage.

     The objective of cost management strategies is to upgrade cost accounting systems so that they produce a financial management information picture. The resulting composite performance measurement structure can be used to drive the decision-making process for product development and pricing, capital investments, and workflows.

Looking for ways to reevaluate how they do business, many managers find that control of costs is critical in reaching bottom-line strategic and financial goals. Practitioners, particularly accounting firms, often position the discipline of cost management as an alternative to touchy-feely strategies, such as total quality management, advocated by some consultants.

Related Terms activity-based costing, balanced scorecard, business process improvement, cost accounting systems, cost drivers, cost of quality, deaveraged profitability analysis, lean production model, life cycle costing, standard costing, target costing, total cost management (TCM)

Examples
- To control the cost of overhead, many U.S. companies have been shifting production sites away from high-cost states such as California to lower-cost states such as Texas where blue-collar labor is plentiful and worker's compensation and state taxes are lower. For example, AST, a desktop computer manufacturer, switched 600 jobs to Fort Worth, Texas, from Orange County in California.
- McDonnell Douglas shifted its helicopter production to Mesa, Arizona, from California to control labor costs.

Suggested Reading
> *Journal of Cost Management.* A Warren, Gorham & Lamont Publication, Editorial Sponsorship by the Consortium for Advanced Manufacturing—International (CAM-I), Boston, Mass.
>
> Ostrenga, Michael R., Terrence R. Ozan, Robert D. McIlhattan, Marcus D. Harwood. *The Ernst & Young Guide to Total Cost Management.* New York: Wiley, 1992.
>
> Uchitelle, Louis. "The New Faces of U.S. Manufacturing." *The New York Times,* July 3, 1994, pp. 3-1, 3-6.

co-venture *See* alliance, partnering/partnerships.

customer-centered organization *See* customer franchise management, customer satisfaction.

customer franchise management (CFM) "The portfolio of customers with whom a firm enjoys a privileged relationship and to whom the firm dedicates its efforts for creating and delivering value." (Bob Wayland of Mercer Management Consulting)

Management of this franchise starts with valuing the customer relationship—its value in hard economic terms—which then allows a company to segment its customers according to the profitability they generate for the firm. This platform gives the company a basis for redefining a marketing system that will include the following elements:

Customer fulfillment: the application of marketing tools and levers across the portfolio to maximize profitability

Customer-centered organization: deploying resources and structuring processes to maximize customer responsiveness

Information management: the use of information to enable customer franchise management strategies

Brand identity management: the identification of customers and their value to the business

Related Terms   customer-centered organization, customer direct access, customer facing strategy, customer fulfillment, customer modeling, customer retention, customer valuation, customerize philosophy[SM], loyalty management, mass customization, point-of-delivery manufacturing, time-based competition, upside-down marketing, zero defections

Examples
- Walgreens, the U.S. retailer, identified high frequency shoppers as its most lucrative customers and subsequently arranged its entire operations, from store format and location to product selection and technology deployment, to fulfilling the needs of this customer franchise.
- Mercer Management Consulting is partnering with Unisys Corporation and *Fortune* magazine on seven business symposia addressing the topics of attracting and keeping customers. Unisys has not only service marked its customerize philosophy[SM], but has also taken out advertising that formally defines its concept of customer satisfaction. Its commitment is to make the company more responsive to its current customers and better able to attract new ones. The philosophy also includes the process of extending a company's information system to branch and field locations to enhance customer service capabilities.

Suggested Reading
Reichheld, Frederick F., and W. Earl Sasser, Jr. "Zero Defections: Quality Comes to Service." *Harvard Business Review,* September–October 1990, pp. 105–111.

Wayland, Robert E. "Customer Valuation: The Foundation of Customer Franchise Management." *Mercer Management Journal,* no. 2, 1994, pp. 45–57.

customerize philosophy[SM]   The Unisys brand name for managing customer relationships. *See* customer franchise management.

customer satisfaction The goal that can integrate the key processes of any business—marketing, engineering, acquisition, manufacturing—in a value network for the company, an effective tool for differentiating one company from another (management consultant Louis DeRose).

Meeting the needs that drive customers to do business with a particular firm—satisfying these customers—is the ultimate objective of every company according to Mack Hanan and Peter Karp. They, among other management gurus, have investigated the dynamics of turning customer satisfaction into profit and a source of competitive advantage—how to measure, manage, and market customer satisfaction.

Related Terms customer franchise management, loyalty management, total customer satisfaction (TCS), TQM, value network

Suggested Reading

DeRose, Louis J. *The Value Network: Integrating the Five Critical Processes That Create Customer Satisfaction.* New York: AMACOM, 1994.

Hanan, Mack, and Peter Karp. *Customer Satisfaction: How to Maximize, Measure, and Market Your Company's "Ultimate Product."* New York: AMACOM, 1991.

deaveraged profitability analysis An analysis of segmented profits and losses that compose the bottom line. Although the phrase may seem clumsy, the concept behind deaveraged profitability is remarkably straightforward. Whereas net income is a fundamental financial measure, deaveraged profitability is an essential analytic discipline that allows a company to peel the onion of internal business performance and gain substantial insights into how profits are being generated.

Conducting a detailed analysis of how a company generates its profitability by building a segmented profit and loss statement by region, line of business, or customer profitability can reveal what a company's core competencies are, whether a partner should be invited in to handle certain aspects of a business, or whether a particular service should be outsourced to an independent supplier.

Lines of business often avoid deaveraging their numbers because of justified concern that the numbers will fail to gain acceptance within the organization. Discussions over allocation methodologies and cost sharing can slow the process and produce reports that may not lead to any management action unless management obtains agreement up front on what the goals of this exercise will be. The purpose of deaveraged profitability analysis should not be to create accounting numbers but rather "good enuf" numbers that the organizational units being analyzed will accept and use as the basis for action.

Related Terms   core competencies, cost management, shareholder value
 analysis

Examples

 • Reengineering or outsourcing of the back office operations functions can be one outcome of a deaveraged profitability study. For
  example, in 1994 American Express Bank, a unit of the American
  Express Company that serves overseas customers, announced that
  it had selected Electronic Data Systems (EDS), an independent
  company that is a unit of General Motors Corp., to provide global
  information management services. Under the contract, EDS was
  reported to be taking on over 200 American Express employees to
  run global operations. American Express said that it expected to
  gain "substantial technical and cost advantages" through the ar-
  rangement.

Suggested Reading

 Wendel, Charles. "Behind the Management Buzzwords." *American
 Banker*, November 29, 1993.

declutter   A British buzzword meaning to focus on the core skills that
 make an enterprise competitive and profitable. *See* core competencies, reengineering.

delayering   The reduction in or elimination of management layers. *See*
 demassing.

demassing   Streamlining program that engineers the removal of large
 numbers of midlevel managers and professionals from a corporation's organization. Often hitting hardest at corporate headquarters
 and resulting in increased decentralization, demassing, a signature
 phrase of Robert Tomasko, can be described as having the following
 five characteristics:

 1. Commitment to large-scale reductions, upward from 5 percent of
  the workforce.
 2. Cutbacks across all departments.
 3. Reductions that impact multiple layers of the organization.
 4. Priority on cutting expenses by lowering headcount to increase
  return on investment.
 5. Fast action within a narrow time frame for achieving reductions.

Related Terms   corporate anorexia, delayering, denominator management, de-organized, disembodied, downsizing, enterprise, harvest
 strategy, rationalization, reductions-in-force, reshaping, restructuring, retrenchment, rightsizing

Examples

 • In 1994, London-based Cable & Wireless P.L.C. announced that it
  planned to cut headquarters staff by 40 percent.

- The 1993 Xerox annual report described employee layoffs as a way of lowering "selling, general, and administrative costs as a percentage of revenue."

Suggested Reading

Stuckey, M. M. *Demassing: Transforming the Dinosaur Corporation.* Portland, Oreg.: Productivity Press, 1993.

Tomasko, Robert M. *Downsizing: Reshaping the Corporation for the Future.* New York: AMACOM, 1990.

denominator management Tactics that include cutting investment and headcount and selling assets to improve performance measurement statistics. The statistics used to measure performance—return on investment (ROI), return on assets (ROA), return on common equity (ROCE), among others—have two components, a numerator that represents net income, and a denominator, which is usually assets, equity, or capital investment. To improve these statistics, managers will often concentrate on the denominators. Cutting investment, assets, and capital employed by cutting headcount and selling assets will show immediate improvements even without an increase in net income. Gary Hamel and C. K. Prahalad, who call this management strategy *denominator management,* see it as a way to sell market share profitably and point out that it will not be favorably received by Wall Street investors unless accompanied by a growth strategy. *See* downsizing, demassing, harvest strategy, management by decree (MBD), numerator management.

de-organized A Tom Peters signature phrase for restructured companies. *See* horizontal corporation.

discontinuous change A radical shift or innovation in the marketplace that dramatically repositions customer expectations and competitive balance. Discontinuous change scenarios can be plotted on a matrix where the y-axis is resistance to change and the x-axis is the force driving change. Paul Strebel, director of the International Executive Program on radical change management at the International Institute for Management Development (IMD) in Lausanne, Switzerland, explains that such dramatic change scenarios play out in the top right hand region of the quadrant "where the rules of competitive behavior in industry change sharply" (Strebel, 1992). If one player changes sides or tactics, the competitive balance is disrupted triggering a "discontinuous change."

Related Terms age of chaos, age of discontinuity, age of paradox, age of unreason, breakpoint, change management, first mover, hypercompetition, paradigm shift, thunderbolt thinking

Examples

- RSA Data Security's introduction of software based on an innovation in cryptography is a breakpoint that has precipitated discontinuous change in the telecommunications marketplace. Guaranteed privacy is now a possibility. The software permits people to exchange messages electronically without previously arranging a code. While it ensures confidentiality, the new system also has no "backdoor" that would allow the U.S. government to eavesdrop on suspected criminals and conduct wiretap investigations for purposes of national security. The U.S. government's angry reaction to this product has placed Jim Bidzos, president of RSA, at the center of a political whirlwind.
- Strebel cites Black Monday, 1987 as an example of discontinuous change. The hint that the U.S. Treasury might change its support of the dollar in late summer 1987 caused a breakpoint for the U.S. stock market, which had been finely balanced between change agents following deteriorating fundamentals and those that had adapted to recent price trends.

Suggested Reading

Drucker, Peter. *The Age of Discontinuity.* New York: Harper & Row, 1969.

Handy, Charles. *The Age of Unreason.* Boston: Harvard Business School Press, 1989.

Strebel, Paul. *Breakpoints: How Managers Exploit Radical Business Change.* Boston: Harvard Business School Press, 1992.

disembodied enterprise   A Tom Peters signature phrase for restructured companies. *See* delayering, demassing, horizontal corporation, virtual corporation.

diversified quality   A term used by German manufacturers to describe producing short, small batches of luxury goods. *See* mass customization, segments of one.

doer model of management   Management practice of a company in which managers join the workers on the line, partly as a way of avoiding the appearance of executive scrutiny. It contrasts to the management system where full-time, lead-bearing managers manage people rather than personally *do* the business. *See* fourth generation management.

doughnut principle   Buzzword image introduced by Charles Handy to help resolve the paradox of work. Also called the inverted doughnut or the inside-out doughnut. Unlike a real doughnut where the hole is in the center, the inverted doughnut has a central core that includes all skills and responsibilities that an individual, a team, or an organization needs to succeed. The surrounding space that rings the doughnut represents those actions/opportunities that differentiate performance. The surrounding space also embodies the broader responsibility to the institution or society that surrounds the essential core.

The image can be used to describe the many kinds of work units that reengineering is now introducing to foster productive corporations, ranging from individual job assignments and work teams to a new shape for the organization itself.

Related Terms core competencies, empowerment, team management, work groups

Examples
- Individuals who have multiple responsibilities but cannot make a decision to spend over $200 without the approval of a superior would have a job described as all core with no space, meaning no ability to use personal judgment.
- Some workers at Ritz Carlton Hotels are empowered to take initiatives, such as opening the health club and the gift shop at unusually early hours, and commit the company to expenditures without seeking a supervisor's approval to ensure the well-being and satisfaction of guests.

Suggested Reading
Handy, Charles. *The Age of Paradox.* Boston: University Press, 1994.

downsizing Defined as across-the-board cost cutting to improve productivity and profitability. Downsizing of staff can be achieved with workforce layoffs, early retirement, and voluntary severance programs.

Related Terms demassing, denominator management, early retirement, reductions-in-force, reengineering, restructuring, retrenchment, rightsizing

Examples
- Critics often ask, "Is downsizing really a successful strategy?" The answer is, "Not always," according to American Management Association (AMA) surveys. Sentiment on downsizing is mixed at as much as half and certainly at least one-third of large and mid-size U.S. companies that have cut their workforces. Among those companies responding to these surveys, only 34 percent of those companies cutting workers reported increases in productivity to the AMA in 1993. Profit improvement was reported by 45 percent, but almost double that number—80 percent—of the downsizing firms admitted that the morale of their employees has plummeted.

- Hewlett-Packard is a preeminent example of a company that has both downsized and remained a vigorous competitor building an empowered workforce. The company approached downsizing as a long-term corporate strategy to pursue renewed growth. Part of Hewlett-Packard's success undoubtedly came from its ability to cut its annual operating expenses without firing a single employee. Early retirement and voluntary severance programs cut expenses and helped preserve employee morale. The programs also redeployed or transferred approximately 5 percent of employees from low-value businesses such as printed circuit boards to high-value ones such as laser printers.
- In a move to counter price discounting and global overcapacity in the paper market, Scott Paper Company announced a downsizing equal to a 25 percent reduction in its workforce. The move was greeted positively by Wall Street sending Scott shares up $2.25 following the announcement.
- New York City began downsizing municipal operations in 1994, targeting a voluntary workforce reduction of 7,500 city employees.

Suggested Reading

Henkoff, Ronald. "Getting Beyond Downsizing." *Fortune,* January 10, 1994, pp. 58–64.

Tomasko, Robert M., *Downsizing: Reshaping the Corporation for the Future.* New York: AMACOM, 1990.

Tomasko, Robert M. *Rethinking the Corporation: The Architecture of Change.* New York: AMACOM, 1993.

drivers   *See* road kill.

economic value added (EVA)   Method for measuring profitability that incorporates a company's cost of capital. A term popularized by Stern Stewart & Co., EVA analysis requires a company and its divisions to determine their "true" cost of capital (COC) companywide as well as the amount of capital tied up in each division.

Simply stated, following the Stern Stewart approach, if the COC is 10 percent and $100 million is required to support investments such as real estate, machinery, working capital, R&D, and training, then $10 million is the annual dollar cost required for capital investments. Managers calculate their EVA by subtracting taxes and the $10 million capital cost from operating earnings. A positive EVA means that an operation creates wealth for the shareholder; a negative number means that it is a value destroyer.

Related Terms   cost management, denominator management, numerator management

Examples
- *Fortune* magazine quotes Quaker Oats CEO William Smithburg, "EVA means managers act like shareholders. It's the true corporate faith for the 1990s."
- After conducting an EVA analysis, CSX, the freight company, reduced its locomotives from 150 to 100 and changed its approach to logistics, a $70 million reduction in capital required to support the business. The CEO of CSX credits EVA with contributing to the rise in the company's stock price.

Suggested Reading
Tully, Shaw. "The Real Key to Creating Wealth." *Fortune,* September 12, 1993, pp. 38–50.

empowerment New type of working environment whereby management gives individuals and/or teams both the power to make decisions and the ability to reward achievement at all levels of an organization. True empowerment requires that management not only inspire trust but also trust its people, who must have the leeway to make mistakes as well as to succeed.

Creating an empowered organization, which can be defined as the process of building a highly committed, decision-making, nonhierarchical workforce, promises a corporation greater competitiveness and profitability by getting employees to go the extra mile.

By empowering employees it is possible to reduce or eliminate extensive bureaucratic structure and effectively manage customer loyalty through the delivery of a quality product or service. Continuous improvement is a goal that can only be reached through an empowered workforce where each employee is accountable to the others. Empowered employees take ownership of their jobs, see themselves as part of the corporation as a whole, and assume personal responsibility for corporatewide performance.

Related Terms adhocracy, bottom-up participation, doughnut principle, employee empowerment, high-performance workplace, intelligent organization, job enrichment, middle-up-down management, participative management, self-leadership, self-management, teams, theory Z

Example
- We often tell the story of a Neiman Marcus salesperson who on her own authority offered to customize a shirt (changing button cuffs to French cuffs) as an example of employee empowerment. While the action cost her and the store some time and a small expense, it produced a profitable sale and the goodwill that leads to future business.

- Semco, a Brazilian manufacturing company, is committed to employee empowerment. In his book *Maverick*, CEO Ricardo Semler explains how his company stresses accountability. Before people are hired or promoted, they are interviewed by everyone who will work for them. Managers are also evaluated every six months by the people who work for them, and the results are posted for all to see.
- In a letter to customers and employees published as a full-page advertisement in *The Wall Street Journal*, Unisys described itself as a company that empowered its employees "with the responsibility to revive" the company.

Suggested Reading

Bennis, Warren, with Burt Nanus. *Leaders: The Strategies of Taking Charge.* New York: Harper & Row, 1985.

Block, Peter. *The Empowered Manager.* San Francisco: Jossey-Bass, 1987.

Byham, William, Ph.D., with Jeff Cox. *Zapp! The Lightning of Empowerment.* New York: Fawcett Columbine, 1988.

Scott, Cynthia D., and Dennis T. Jaffe. *Empowerment: A Practical Guide for Success.* Menlo Park, Calif.: Crisp Publications, 1991.

Semler, Ricardo. *Maverick: The Success Story Behind the World's Most Unusual Workplace.* New York: Warner Books, 1993.

end products   Finished or commodity products marketed to the public, not the core business of a corporate enterprise. Usually, end products are the result of one or more core competencies and are assembled from the components described as core products. The term was popularized by Gary Hamel and C. K. Prahalad.

Related Terms   core competencies, core products, strategic architecture

Examples

- Despite a reported 84 percent of the world market share in desktop laser printer engines, a core component of these printers, Canon has only a small share of the market for the printers themselves, which are described as end products.
- 3M has reportedly leveraged 16 core technologies into 60,000 end products sold to customers.

Suggested Reading

Prahalad, C. K., and Gary Hamel. "The Core Competence of the Corporation." *Harvard Business Review,* vol. 68, no. 3, May–June 1990, pp. 79–91.

enterprise management   *see* enterprise unit.

enterprise unit   A component of the horizontal corporation that performs only those business activities essential to maintaining competitive standing. This unit contrasts to the SBU, which conducts all functions, allowing it to stand alone as an independent unit. *See* core products, federalism.

excellence   Signature phrase of Tom Peters and Robert Waterman for companies that demonstrate outstanding industry leadership.

federalism   Describes the paradox that allows business to be centralized and decentralized as well as local and global at the same time. This Jeffersonian term describing the ideal state and federal government balance of power has been introduced to the business world both by Warren Bennis and by Charles Handy.

Two key concepts of business federalism as described by Handy are twin citizenship and subsidiarity. Twin citizenship views the individual worker as belonging to two groups, the larger company and the smaller work unit. Subsidiarity is the direct opposite of hierarchical delegation of authority. The term describes how subsidiary teams of workers at the job site are empowered to make immediate decisions on how to accomplish a task and then delegate responsibility outward to a central administration that provides such infrastructure support as capital and information systems.

Related Terms   borderless organization, boundaryless organization, bunsha, empowerment, enterprise unit, horizontal corporation, PALs (pooling, allying, linking companies), participative management, subsidiarity, virtual corporation

Examples

- Warren Bennis described Coca-Cola CEO Robert Goizueta as the "sharpest image of the new federal leader that comes to mind" because as a leader of leaders he unites his associates by establishing a climate and structure that gives all members of the organization a sense of purpose and vision.
- The form of a federalist organization has applications for both manufacturing and service industries. The American Airlines SABRE system links small and large competitors in the airline industry.
- Asea Brown Boveri (ABB) is described by Warren Bennis as an example of "federalism with a vengeance." The company, the largest power engineering group in the world, has more employees than the population of Iceland, is divided into nearly 1,200 companies and 5,000 profit centers, but has only 100 professionals at its Zurich headquarters. Percy Barnevik, the chief executive, has eliminated intermediate management control layers and pushed responsibility into the operating units.

- Before current Chairman Lou Gerstner took over the helm, *The New York Times* reported that IBM was pursuing a plan to give each of its businesses greater autonomy. Separate financial statements were being created for this "IBM federation of businesses" with the aim of selling them off as stand-alone companies. Gerstner reversed this strategy and decided to keep IBM together as a single enterprise.

Suggested Reading

Bennis, Warren. *An Invented Life: Reflections on Leadership and Change.* Reading, Mass.: Addison-Wesley, 1993.

Lohr, Steve. "On the Road With Chairman Lou." *The New York Times,* Sunday, June 26, 1994, pp. 3-1, 3-6.

fifth discipline   *See* learning organization.

fifth generation management   Management system based on human networking. An organizational consultant with Digital Equipment Corporation, Charles Savage, like Peter Senge (*see* learning organization), draws parallels from the fifth generation of computer networks to the management of human organizations.

Savage projects that a fifth generation management organization will evolve where human networks will use computer technology to leverage collective knowledge. In building his analogy, he states that in the early 1980s, the Japanese Ministry for International Trade and Industry (MITI) launched a fifth generation computer project; it was followed by similar enterprises in the United States and in Europe. The first four generations of computers all pass information through a single central processing unit (CPU) which has been described as the von Neumann bottleneck (named after the mathematician and computer pioneer). The key to fifth generation computer management, parallel processing, requires the networking of multiple processing units that can work on the same problem simultaneously and significantly speed up analysis. Networking further allows multiple applications in parallel on different computers by linking databases and allowing multiple users.

Just as computer processing had reached a bottleneck, Savage sees the first four generations of management, which are the creation of the industrial era—proprietorships, steep hierarchies, matrix management, and computer interfacing—as reaching an impasse. The next step is fifth generation management which he calls "human networking."

As a consultant, Savage is applying the basic concepts of the knowledge-creating organization to describe the evolution taking place in business management.

Related Terms fourth generation management, knowledge-creating company, learning organization, reengineering, time-based competition, TQM (total quality management), wired company

Examples
- Asea Brown Boveri (ABB), the world's largest power engineering group, has chosen the U.S. dollar as its currency of reporting and English as its common language, even though only a minority of its employees call English their mother tongue. The objective is to facilitate the human network and develop common values.

Suggested Reading
> Drucker, Peter. "The Coming of the New Organization." *Harvard Business Review*, January–February 1988, pp. 45–53.
> Nolan, Richard, Alex J. Pollock, and James P. Ware. "Creating the 21st Century Organization." *Stage by Stage 8:4*. Lexington, Mass.: Nolan, Norton and Co., Fall 1988, p. 11.
> Nolan, Richard, Alex J. Pollock, and James P. Ware. "Toward the Design of Network Organizations." *Stage by Stage 9:1.* Lexington, Mass.: Nolan, Norton and Co., Fall 1988, pp. 1–12.
> Savage, Charles M. *Fifth Generation Management: Integration of Enterprises Through Human Networking.* Cambridge, Mass.: Digital Press, 1990.

first mover Strategic term, introduced by Michael Porter, describing how a company gains competitive advantage by being the first to introduce a new product or service. *See* discontinuous change, gazelle, hypercompetition, sur/petition.

flexible management Involves companies employing small business craftspeople as part of their contingent workforce. This practice gives the larger company the ability to leverage the advantages offered by its size, such as economy of scale and sophisticated marketing skills, while keeping overhead low.

Related Terms accordion management, agile management, contingent workforce, lean production model, mass customization

Example
- Benetton uses its relationships with a multitude of suppliers to meet consumers' fast changing interest in style.

Suggested Reading
> Applebaum, Eileen, and Rosemary Batt. *The New American Workplace.* Ithaca, N.Y.: ILR Press, 1994.
> Harrison, Bennett. *Lean and Mean: The Changing Landscape of Corporate Power in the Age of Flexibility.* New York: BasicBooks, 1994.

followership   "The people who know what to do without being told" (Robert Kelley, 1991). Kelley, who teaches a course called Followership and Leadership for Professional Effectiveness in the Industrial Management Program at the Graduate School of Industrial Administration of Carnegie-Mellon University, claims that 80 percent of the success of any project is due to the followers and that only 20 percent to the contribution of leaders.

Kelley describes followers not as sheep but as collaborators, empowered individuals who can act without being told what to do, who can make informed decisions based on "intelligence, independence, courage, and a strong sense of ethics."

Related Terms   apprentice, bottom-up participation, comrade, disciple, empowerment, mentee, self-leadership, self-management, team management

Examples
  • Eastman Chemical, a unit of Kodak, eliminated the post of senior vice president for administration, manufacturing, and now has over 1,000 self-directed work teams.

Suggested Reading
  DePree, Max. *Leadership Is an Art.* New York: Dell Publishing, 1989.
  Kelley, Robert. "In Praise of Followers." *Harvard Business Review*, November–December 1988, pp. 142–148.
  Kelley, Robert. *The Power of Followership.* New York: Doubleday, 1991.

fourth generation management   Unified vision or system for business leaders. Drawing together a variety of ideas that inspired the total quality movement, visionary leadership theories, reengineering, and time-based competition among other theories, Brian Joiner has presented what he calls "fourth generation management." Although Joiner's book was published after Charles Savage's *Fifth Generation Management*, they approach the subject of management from different angles. Joiner describes the four generations of management as:

1st Generation: Management by Doing. In the first generation of management the "manager" does the task himself or herself. Capacity and productivity under this system are, of course, limited.

2nd Generation: Management by Directing. This system allows experts to micromanage, leveraging their influence by giving strict instructions on how to accomplish a task and what standards should be maintained.

3rd Generation: Management by Results. Under this management system, the workforce is given quotas or targets and told to figure out the methodology for accomplishing the task independently.

4th Generation Management. Under fourth generation management, the customer's needs come first, the organization is viewed as a system, process thinking is stressed, and everyone in the organization is treated with respect. Joiner's management system is strongly influenced by W. Edwards Deming's theories concerning how knowledge should be used in management. The three key elements of fourth generation management, as Joiner describes them, are:
  - A dedication to quality, as the customer defines it
  - A scientific approach to rapid learning
  - Creation of team relationships both inside and beyond the business organization

Related Terms   doer model of management, empowerment, fifth generation management, reengineering, time-based competition, TQM (total quality management)

Examples
  - An example of management by results would be when salespersons are given quotas without the training and infrastructure support necessary for success.
  - While Joiner provides no named examples, one fourth generation management company might be GFC Financial Corporation, which surveys customers to ensure quality and responsiveness, invests heavily in training, and encourages teaming within the company by a number of methods, including compensation plans and making all employees shareholders.

Suggested Reading
  Joiner, Brian L. *Fourth Generation Management: The New Business Consciousness.* New York: McGraw-Hill, 1994.

gainsharing   Practice of having employees share directly in a company's gain or profitability. *See* pay for performance.

gazelle   Not simply a fast-growing company but a *volatile* company that may demonstrate a growth rate of as much as 20 percent per year because it is willing to enter new markets with new products ahead of the pack. There are approximately 500,000 of these companies in America, according to *Biz* magazine. Gazelles have a median age of 15 years, and one in four gazelle employees work for firms that have been in business for over 30 years, according to Cognetics Inc., an economic research firm. *The Economist* reports that gazelles are responsible for 70 percent of America's job growth, although only 3 percent of the private sector's payroll.

Related Terms   discontinuous change, entrepreneurship, first mover, hypercompetition, sur/petition

Example
- In March 1994, *Biz* magazine, a joint venture between Dow Jones and American City Business Journals Inc., identified its target readership as the gazelles, America's 500,000 fastest-growing businesses. The magazine announced this strategy in a full-page *Wall Street Journal* advertisement and offered a free copy of its publication to these 500,000 companies.

Suggested Reading
Birch, David, Anne Haggerty, and William Parsons. *Corporate Almanac 1994.* Cambridge, Mass.: Cognetics Inc., 1994.

Biz Magazine advertisement. *The Wall Street Journal,* March 12, 1994, p. B12.

"Bounding Gazelles." *The Economist,* May 28, 1994, p. 65.

globalization   A "widening and deepening of companies' operations across borders to produce and sell goods and services in more markets" (The Organization for Economic Cooperation and Development [OECD]).

Related Terms   alliances, borderless organization, boundaryless organization, global webs, PALs, partnering, triad power

Examples
- The globalization trend fueled the outflow of foreign direct investment in the late 1980s. Between 1983 and 1989, the average annual increase in foreign direct investment was 29 percent, or three times faster than trade and four times faster than world economic growth, according to *The Financial Times.*
- ABB (Asea Brown Boveri) is often cited as the model for the multinational industrial corporation of the global marketplace. The company has introduced a common set of values policies and guidelines to ensure a groupwide umbrella culture, according to Chief Executive Percy Barnevik.

Suggested Reading
Norman, Peter. "Economics Notebook: Employment Challenge." *The Financial Times,* June 1994.

Roger, Ian. "The Inside Story of a Model Multinational." *The Financial Times,* June 27, 1994, p. 9.

growth   A new buzzword describing the potential, positive business result of reengineering. How to become a more profitable market leader in the new economy of the 1990s is a hot topic as businesses emerge from the cost-cutting, pink-slip orgies of downsizing. Management consulting firms, the management gurus, and business journalists are all exploring the factors that contribute to what Gary

Hamel and C. K. Prahalad call the ability to create "fundamentally new competitive space" and effectively use resources and imagine new products and industries.

Suggestions for new ways of thinking and promoting growth range across a broad spectrum from rationale strategies for structuring better sales channel management to radical ways of sponsoring in-house innovation and creativity.

Andrew Serwer of *Fortune* has identified five lessons taught by the new growth companies, which are typically smaller than the growth leaders of a decade ago and are often run by independent-minded entrepreneurs willing to try the new management techniques. These lessons are:

1. Keep experimenting.
2. Accept failure as part of the process.
3. Identify competitors' "religious" behavior—what is sacred to them—and take advantage of it.
4. Women entrepreneurs are more like men entrepreneurs than they are like other women.
5. Would-be entrepreneurs who sit and wait for the great idea are destined to fail.

Related Terms   alliance, channels management, customer franchise management, gazelle, industry foresight, intrapreneuring, partnerships, triad power

Examples

- Grow Biz International, number one on the *Fortune* list of the Top 100 growth companies, has an annual (three- to five-year) growth rate of 285 percent.
- Boston Chicken is often cited as an outstanding growth company. Willing to experiment, the company sees itself as in the "home-cooked meal replacement business" and nurtures antihierarchical organization behavior to promote collaboration and teamwork.
- John Byrne, senior writer at *Business Week,* has identified global growth as the focus and fuel for the expansion of the large management consulting firms such as McKinsey & Company over the next decade.

Suggested Reading

Aley, James, and Vivian Brownstein. "Where to Find Fast Growth." *Fortune,* September 5, 1994, vol. 130, no. 5, p. 25.

Douthwaite, Richard. *The Growth Illusion: How Economic Growth Has Enriched the Few, Impoverished the Many, and Endangered the Planet.* Tulsa, Okla.: Oak Books, 1993.

Hamel, Gary, and C. K. Prahalad. *Competing for the Future: Break-*

through Strategies for Seizing Control of Your Industry and Creating the Markets of Tomorrow. Boston: Harvard Business School Press, 1994.
Serwer, Andrew E. "Lessons From America's Fastest Growing Companies." *Fortune,* August 8, 1994, vol. 130, no. 5, pp. 42–60.

harvest strategy Term used by Gary Hamel and C. K. Prahalad in their discussion of competitive strategies. If a company aggressively reduces investments, assets, or capital employed while the revenue stream remains flat, it can sell or harvest its market share. Productivity will increase dramatically even if manufacturing output also remains flat. *See* demassing, denominator management, downsizing, rightsizing.

high-performance involvement *See* high-performance workplace.

high-performance workplace (HPW) A reaction to the migration of mass-produced products to the developing countries. The goal of the HPW is to use information technology to move away from mass production and produce value-added products and services by improving efficiency and quality. The concept is a broad one that has different interpretations in the developed countries.

Related Terms diversified quality, empowerment, fifth generation management, high-performance work systems, high-performance teams, informationalization, lean production, mass customization, quality circles, total quality management

Examples
- Federal Express's use of technology and tracking software has propelled it into the top ranks of courier services worldwide, creating a high-performance workplace.
- When Citicorp gave almost every employee in its Canadian Real Estate Group a multifunction workstation, allowing access to a wide range of information databases inside and outside the company, the implementation of this work-group computing strategy had a significant impact on productivity and reportedly translated into bottom-line benefits. Redesign of the business processes using technology created a high-performance workplace where executive time spent on administration dropped while marketing time increased, resulting in profit center earnings more than doubling (Tapscott and Caston, 1993).

Suggested Reading
Katzenbach, Jon R., and Douglas K. Smith. *The Wisdom of Teams: Creating the High Performance Organization.* Boston, Mass.: Harvard Business School Press, 1993.

Tapscott, Don, and Art Caston. *Paradigm Shift: The New Promise of Information Technology.* New York: McGraw-Hill, 1993.

high-performance work systems   *See* high-performance workplace.

horizontal corporation   The result when a company reduces hierarchy, breaks its organization into units that reflect its core processes, and creates cross-functional teams made up of members from different departments to run them.

   This organization structure is the antithesis of the vertical corporation that doles out information sparingly in tightly controlled channels. The horizontal corporate world, in contrast, is networked internally and focused outward toward its customers. Hierarchical and department boundaries are eliminated, supervision is minimized, and self-managing teams accountable for a common purpose become the building blocks of the new enterprise.

Related Terms   borderless organization, boundaryless organization, BPR, buckyborgs, core processes, customer-driven management, de-organized, disembodied enterprise, empowerment, high-performance workplace, horizontal management, inverted pyramid, shamrock organization, virtual corporation

Examples
- Xerox uses multidisciplinary teams to manage new product development rather than vertical functions or departments.
- At General Electric, Chairman John Welch, Jr., talks about building a "boundaryless" organization that will increase GE's ability to respond to customers.
- Very few organization charts of established corporations currently present a picture of a horizontal organization. Start-up companies, however, have the option to structure themselves horizontally. Astra/Merck Group, a stand-alone company created by Merck to market antiulcer and high blood pressure drugs, has organized itself around market-driven business processes such as drug development and distribution, creating a structure that mirrors its customer focus.

Suggested Reading

Byrne, John A. "The Horizontal Corporation." *Business Week*, December 20, 1993, pp. 76–83.

Davidow, William H., and Michael S. Malone. *The Virtual Corporation: Structuring and Revitalizing the Corporation for the 21st Century.* New York: HarperBusiness, 1992.

Peters, Tom. *The Tom Peters Seminar: Crazy Times Call for Crazy Organizations.* New York: Vintage, 1994.

Waterman, Robert. *What America Does Right: Learning From Companies That Put People First.* New York: Norton, 1994.

hoteling   A premises management strategy that allows firms to cut space requirements and bottom-line expenses by creating a direct link between actual need and physical use of office space. This office housing concept is most effective at accounting, consulting, or sales-oriented firms where employees spend a large portion of their time on the road or at the client's office.

Rather than being assigned a permanent office, employees who frequently travel request space when they need to attend a meeting at the office or are concentrating on getting new business, similar to booking a hotel room. Between visits to the office, employees stay in touch with management by E-mail and voice mail. Data that needs to be shared can be downloaded, and software that is needed for a project can be accessed via modem. Personal belongings are stored in a locker, and cubicles are assigned by a hoteling administrator who acts as a concierge, handling details such as programming phones and placing names on the door.

Hoteling is the characteristic housing choice of the virtual office.

The drawback of this extremely cost-effective program is that employees rarely get to know anyone at the firm unless they work with them on an off-site project. Office space may be scarce and crowded, occasionally requiring that several people work in a conference room. Some employees say they miss having a home-away-from-home and a place to work on the weekends.

Related Terms   virtual office, wired company, wired executive

Examples
- Ernst & Young has pursued the concept of hoteling in its San Francisco, Chicago, and New York offices. The accounting firm estimates that it will save approximately $40 million a year in expenses when the program is in place nationwide and has already reduced office space by approximately 25 percent. The concept of having one office for every three consultants is particularly well suited to the auditing and consulting industry where employees often work at clients' offices four or five days a week.
- *Business Week* magazine offers an executive program entitled The Realities of the Virtual Office, in association with MicroAge Infosystems Services and AT&T Global Information Solutions. The program gives managers an overview of how to integrate portable computers and telecommunications into their business strategies.

Suggested Reading

Gunsch, Dawn. "Turning Office Space Into a Hotel." *Personnel Journal,* vol. 71, no. 11, November 1992, pp. 16–19.

Patton, Phil. "The Virtual Office Becomes a Reality." *The New York Times*, October 28, 1993, p. C1.

Sprout, Alison L. "Moving Into the Virtual Office." *Fortune*, May 2, 1994, p. 103.

human networking   Signature phrase of Charles Savage that describes the web of human relationships in the information-age corporation. Gifford and Elizabeth Pinchot use a similar phrase to describe human relationships in the intelligent organization. *See* fifth generation management, intelligent organization, wired company.

hypercompetition   Rapid moves and countermoves that have escalated the pace of strategic change. Traditional sources of competitive advantage are not sustainable given today's dynamic marketplace. This business imperative inspired Richard D'Aveni to incorporate the ideas of many contemporary business theorists and create a new buzzword—hypercompetition.

To explore the rules of this dynamic marketplace, D'Aveni developed an operational model that defines four battlegrounds of competition:

- Price and quality
- Timing and know-how
- Stronghold creation invasion
- Deep pockets

Companies that become winners on this turf are as bold and as aggressive as they are innovative; they continually disrupt the status quo and seize the initiative in these arenas to grab a temporary competitive advantage.

Related Terms   breakpoint, discontinuous change, first mover, hyperfast product development, innovation, gazelle, paradigm shift, s-curve analysis, sur/petition

Examples
- *Business Week* has described Microsoft as a hypercompetitive firm, using its dominance in operating systems as a springboard to launch new applications programs and then quickly moving into the next generation of programming, even before the cycle has run its course, to preempt the competition.
- *Business Week* also described the airline industry as being in a state of hypercompetition, seeking temporary competitive advantage through such maneuvers as frequent flyer miles, roomier seating, video monitors, and special services for business-class flyers.
- Product innovations in the computer industry and car design may

be expected, given the rapid development of technology. D'Aveni also cites product innovation as the source of disruption to the hot sauce industry, a slow-cycle, stable industry which has shown little change for the past century. McIlhenny's Tabasco sauce had a 125-year hold on this market until the introduction of new flavors by companies such as Red Hot weakened the flavor lock and diluted Tabasco's market share.

Suggested Reading

D'Aveni, Richard A., with Robert Gunther. *Hypercompetition: Managing the Dynamics of Strategic Maneuvering.* New York: The Free Press, 1994.

Rebollo, Kathy. "Microsoft: Bill Gates' Baby Is on Top of the World. Can It Stay There?" *Business Week,* February 24, 1992, pp. 62–64.

Zellner, Wendy, and Andrea Rothman. "The Airline Mess." *Business Week,* July 6, 1993, p. 50.

hyperfast product development *See* hypercompetition, time-based competition.

imaginization Creative problem-solving system for use in business organizations conceived by Gareth Morgan. Imaginization challenges traditional mental models and theories by asking individuals to visualize images of objects or living creatures that convey the essence of a person, an organization, or a process. The objective, according to Morgan, is to foster a new dialogue free from bureaucratic and emotional constraints, one that looks to the physical world for analogies and innovative solutions to problems.

Related Terms knowledge-creating company, lateral thinking

Examples

- Gareth Morgan relays the story that while discussing structures for a new educational organization, he hit upon the image of the spider plant to convey the sense of "organic growth in a local environment."

- Another example of imaginization would be for an employee who is asked to provide feedback on a manager to describe that person as a hedgehog, conveying the image that she is easily offended (prickly) and keeps emotions close to the vest. By using the imagery, the employee can shift the dialogue out of the realm of personal attack and concentrate the discussion on behavior.

Suggested Reading

Morgan, Gareth. *Imaginization: The Art of Creative Management.* U.K.: Sage, 1993.

industry foresight   The proactive ability to imagine the future of tomorrow's markets and discover new competitive space, escaping the myopia of the current served market. Gary Hamel and C. K. Prahalad contrast industry foresight to vision. They say industry foresight starts with an idea of what could be and then works backward to what must happen for that future to become a reality.

Related Terms   intellectual capital, intellectual property, knowledge-creating company, managerial frame, opportunity arena, opportunity horizon, renewal factor, wallenda factor

Examples
- Hamel and Prahalad give Motorola's pursuit of satellite-based personal communications and JVC's commitment to the VCR as examples of industry foresight.
- Buffets, Inc., a restaurant chain, claims to have changed the restaurant industry, according to founder Roe Hatlen. The eateries sell one-price, all-you-can-eat meals served buffet style.

Suggested Reading
Hamel, Gary, and C. K. Prahalad. *Competing for the Future: Breakthrough Strategies for Seizing Control of Your Industry and Creating the Markets of Tomorrow.* Boston: Harvard Business School Press, 1994.

informated company   A company wired by technology and flooded with information. Harvard Business School Professor Shoshana Zuboff, who is studying companies that employ technology to change the nature of work, presents a philosophical and somewhat dark vision of the "informated company."

Zuboff sees a future where informated companies face a dilemma: Do they use information and technology to defend management authority and consciously or unconsciously deskill and demotivate the workforce? Or, does this company of the future develop a strategy that uses the information it now possesses to encourage knowledge and learning to motivate its workforce?

Related Terms   fifth generation management, informationalize, learning organization, wired company

Examples
- Zuboff's popularity on the management guru speaking circuit attests to the number of companies that are actively considering the impact of technology and the flood of available information on the workforce. Her book *In the Age of the Smart Machine* is still in print years after publication, a further indication of the depth of interest in the problems she discusses.
- In 1994, *Fortune* ran several cover stories on the wired company

and the new economy created by information technology. Their interpretation is less dark than Zuboff's vision, perhaps because corporate America has become more comfortable with information technology in the intervening six years since Zuboff's book was published.

- On March 14, 1994, Pitney Bowes executive John Manzo issued a Freedom of Information Act to his staff that promised them the "inalienable right to whatever information you need to do your job."

Suggested Reading

Zuboff, Shoshana. *In the Age of the Smart Machine.* New York: BasicBooks, 1988.

informationalize To outpace the competition creating new products and services that are based on the economic value of using and selling information. The discipline of informationalization can redefine competitive dynamics based on data captured about the habits and preferences of customers and can use information technology to create or revitalize an existing product or service and to cut costs.

Related Terms channels marketing, info-marketing, informated company, sur/petition, valufacture

Examples

- Chase Manhattan Bank has used information technology and an understanding of the business needs of corporations to create a corporate credit card that can be used in purchasing small-ticket items. The purchasing card will help companies both reduce costs and speed up the cumbersome paper-intensive purchasing process.

- P&G is standardizing and streamlining the way retailers pay for and receive shipments of its products. By automating its information database, P&G reportedly projects cutting its own costs by eliminating manual correction of orders. By cutting the number of paper invoices customers handle by 25 to 75 percent, the company said it would save between $35 and $75 per invoice.

- Fingerhut, the Minneapolis-based mail order company, built a sophisticated credit system to manage its low-income customer base. The company then realized that credit data is also an excellent source of behavioral information when paired with purchase analysis to allow precise targeting of sales campaigns.

Suggested Reading

Davis, Stan. *2020 Vision: Transform Your Business Today to Succeed in Tomorrow's Economy.* New York: Simon & Schuster, 1991.

Heygate, Richard. "Technophobes, Don't Run Away Just Yet." *The Wall Street Journal,* August 15, 1994, p. A-10.

information partnership A Robert Tomasko signature phrase. *See* Chapter 2: Behind the Buzzwords: The Gurus of Change Management.

insiderization A signature phrase of Kenichi Ohmae that describes a company becoming an insider in a country important to its market share growth through an alliance or partnership.

insourcing New buzzword that has grown in use due to an opposition to outsourcing and has two meanings.

First, insourcing means the retention of a service "inside" the company, keeping a department intact with full-time staff.

Second, insourcing can mean the setting up of a semi-independent service unit inside the company that sells services to in-house users. These users then negotiate directly with the support area for the purchase of services, agreeing on the amounts to be charged. *See* Keyes, 1993, in Selected Bibliography; activity value analysis; outsourcing.

intellectual capital Signature phrase of Warren Bennis that describes the ideas and knowledge offered by key employees that make a company competitive. *See* core competencies, industry foresight.

intellectual leadership *See* post-heroic leadership, strategic architecture.

intellectual property The product of intellectual capital. *See* industry foresight, intellectual capital.

intelligent organization Postbureaucratic organization of the future. Warren Bennis credits Elizabeth and Gifford Pinchot as the source of this serendipitous term. These management gurus envision a future in which leaders will cultivate the intelligence of every member and encourage a shared vision.

To leave behind the bureaucratic systems of organization, the Pinchots advocate structural change that "rebuilds the pattern of relationships and the quality of communications in the organization on the basis of freedom and rights." The resulting human network of groups and individuals will create what the Pinchots describe as "the organization's brain."

The Pinchots link the "intelligent organization" closely with their concept of intrapreneurship.

Related Terms adhocracy, empowerment, fifth generation management, followership, high-performance workplace, human network, intrapreneurship, knowledge-creating company, learning organization, participative management, perpetual entrepreneurship, teams, wired company

Examples
- 3M empowers people at every level and, as part of its commitment to its workers' intelligence, uses self-forming, cross-disciplinary teams to screen new product ideas. New concepts must first be sold to a group of peers, a process that both encourages teamwork and builds organizational intelligence. The company manages over sixty thousand products, attesting to the success of this process.
- Hewlett-Packard is also cited by the Pinchots as an intelligent organization meeting the challenges of a changing marketplace. In its transition from an instrument business to a computer business in the late 1970s and early 1980s, Hewlett-Packard first tried a consensus management approach built on committee decision making. When the company found that this bureaucracy slowed the development process, it abolished many committees and made a commitment to become a decentralized company relying on the intelligence of divisions to make the right decisions for the businesses that they run.

Suggested Reading
    Pinchot, Gifford, and Elizabeth Pinchot. *The End of Bureaucracy and The Rise of the Intelligent Organization.* San Francisco: Berrett-Koehler Publishers, Inc., 1993.

intracapital   The fund or grant set aside by corporations for use by intrapreneurs in pursuing an innovative project on behalf of the corporation. *See* intrapreneuring.

intrapreneuring   Concept that suggests that you do not have to leave the corporation to become an entrepreneur (Pinchot, 1985). The idea advocates combining the advantages of a large firm's resources with the independence and creativity of a small venture.

Related Terms   corporateur, insourcing, intracapital, intraprises, perpetual entrepreneurship

Examples
- In the preface of his book *Intrapreneuring*, Gifford Pinchot lists an honor roll of individuals who played a key role in business innovation inside their corporations. Among those honored are Hulki Aldikacti for the Pontiac Fiero sports car and P. D. Estridge for IBM's personal computer.
- Post-it notes, manufactured by 3M, are a classic and often-cited example of intrapreneurship. Art Fry, the inventor and intrapren-

eur who also sang in a church choir, started the project seeking a peelable marker that would not damage his hymnal. Fry relentlessly pursued his idea searching for the proper adhesive and production machinery. When the manufacturing engineering function at 3M said the machine he had designed would take six months to build and cost a small fortune, Fry built a crude version of the machine at home and got the process up and running overnight (Pinchot, 1985).

Suggested Reading
Brown, Tom. "Farewell to the Furious '80s." *Industry Week,* January 8, 1990, p. 59.

Pinchot, Gifford, III. *Intrapreneuring: Why You Don't Have to Leave the Corporation to Become an Entrepreneur.* New York: Harper & Row, 1985.

just-in-time (JIT) production   Process that requires keeping just enough inventory on hand to meet manufacturing needs for periods as short as four hours. The process-oriented system cuts inventory costs but requires excellent relationships with suppliers who must be linked into the production process by computer. The Japanese term *kanban* is translated as just-in-time manufacture or production and abbreviated as JIT.

The advantage of successful JIT systems is that they help a company to run on zero working capital. Every one dollar freed from inventories rings up a one dollar contribution to cash flow. There is also a permanent contribution to savings; as inventories disappear, companies no longer need warehouses or the staff to run them.

The drawback to just-in-time systems centers on how to anticipate sudden surges. Forecasts are extrapolated from old trends, and highly sophisticated techniques are required to work in a dynamic economy where the relationships of economic variables are in constant flux. Companies that follow just-in-time procedures may be forced to add costly overtime or hire temporary personnel to catch up with market demand or miss the cycle entirely.

Some critics of the JIT process claim that major corporations are essentially transferring the costs of carrying inventory to their suppliers who must keep the necessary materials on hand to keep the business relationship active.

Related Terms   activity-based costing, complexification, empowerment, *kanban, kaizen* (continuous improvement), you-carry-my-inventory, zero working capital

Examples
- At its Adam Opel plant in Eisenach, Germany, General Motors intensively trains workers for JIT management. JIT parts delivery

allows GM to keep just four to six hours' worth of parts in the plant and only two hours' worth of inventory along an uncluttered assembly line. Computer links to suppliers, such as Lear Seating, transmit assembly schedules hours in advance, allowing suppliers time to manufacture and make parts hours before delivery. Along with flexible teams of workers and an emphasis on continuous improvement *(kaizen)* this strategy is dramatically improving productivity at GM's East European plant.

- McGraw-Hill, Inc., publishers has had a computer system in place since 1989 that allows it to order and print books locally on demand, doing away with the need to stock extra books in warehouses and cutting overhead costs.

Suggested Reading

Ansari, A., and B. Modarress. *Just-in-Time Purchasing.* New York: Free Press, 1990.

Tully, Shawn. "Raiding a Company's Hidden Cash." *Fortune,* vol. 130, no. 4, August 22, 1994, pp. 82–89.

kaizen   *See* continuous improvement.

kanban   Japanese term for the just-in-time (JIT) delivery process used in the supply, manufacturing, distribution, and retailing of products. The term was derived from the *kanban* order cards used to request parts from another team on Japanese production lines. *See* just-in-time production.

kanbrain   The just-in-time delivery of brain power. Just as the concept of *kanban*—just-in-time supply, manufacture, and distribution—slashed inventories and transformed the manufacturing process, networked personal computers are transforming corporate training departments. According to *Forbes* writer Lewis Perelman, *kanbrain* promises to have a radical impact on how businesses share information with employees.

At the core of this new concept for a learning infrastructure is the rapid spread of performance support systems, software tools that deliver knowledge to users online or just-in-time while they are doing their jobs.

Related Terms   brainware, fifth discipline, just-in-time intelligence, informated company, *kanban,* performance support systems, learning organization, on-demand hyperlearning

Examples

- *Forbes* reports that Andersen Consulting has developed Knowledge Xchange, an interactive LAN network that creates an electronic marketplace or a "community of practice" where the firm's

27,000 consultants can share their knowledge and expertise. Using their desktop and laptop computers, consultants can log on to keep up to date on discussion topics and their peers' work.

- The interactive network introduced by Hewlett-Packard (HP) to train sales representatives has been so successful—cutting the cost of attending training seminars more than a reported 98 percent—that the service is being sold to other institutions. Rather than attending classroom training at a central location, the HP sales representatives now access training via a teleconference. Training courses are beamed live to HP conference rooms worldwide, and "students" communicate with instructors via voice and computer transmission. HP plans to add video servers to facilitate on-demand training, further transforming the learning process.

Suggested Reading
Perelman, Lewis J. "Kanban to Kanbrain." *Forbes ASAP,* June 6, 1994, pp. 84–85.

keiretsu Japanese conglomerates. The intricate web of relationships that links many different types of companies in these conglomerates, from the Japanese government itself, to banks, suppliers, distributors, and manufacturers, has often been cited as the driving force behind Japan's industrial strength.

Related Terms alliance, *chaebol* (the South Korean conglomerates), partnering, virtual corporation

Examples
- Kenichi Miyashita and David Russell divide the *keiretsu* into three types:

   Horizontal keiretsu, the bank-centered big six, including the Sanwa and Dai-Ichi Kangyo Bank Groups

   Vertical keiretsu, the producers of cars, such as Toyota and Nissan, and electronics, such as Matsushita, and their subcontractors

   Distribution keiretsu that control Japanese retailing

Suggested Reading
Johnson, Hazel J. *The Banking Keiretsu.* Chicago: Probus Publishing, 1993.

Miyashita, Kenichi, and David Russell. *Keiretsu: Inside the Hidden Japanese Conglomerates.* New York: McGraw-Hill, 1994.

knowledge-creating company An enterprise that uses metaphors and analogies to foster and encourage new interpretations of available data. To nurture the process of product innovation, Japanese companies frequently use figurative language that can also be described as slogans or metaphors to jump start the creative process. Honda, for example, used "Theory of Automobile Evolution" as the slogan for generating the design concept for a new car.

Ikujiro Nonaka, a professor of management at Hitosubashi University in Tokyo describes business organizations that adopt this approach to development and are committed to continuous innovation as "knowledge-creating companies." These organizations, according to Nonaka, become famous for their ability to respond quickly to customers, create new markets, and develop new products that exploit emerging technologies.

Rather than taking a narrow view of knowledge as systematic data that is codified, knowledge-creating companies adopt a holistic, nonstop approach to innovation. Using metaphors to link seemingly contradictory ideas, analogies to resolve the contradictions, and, finally, models to crystallize the concepts and make the knowledge available to others, these companies transform tacit ideas into reality; they also continually recreate the organization according to a particular vision or what Nonaka calls an "ideal." The key to this process is tapping into individual employee creativity and commitment to innovation.

Related Terms continuous innovation, fifth discipline, intelligent organization, lateral thinking, learning organization, paradigm shift, time-based competition

Examples

- Nonaka cites a number of Japanese companies, including Honda, Canon, NEX, and Matsushita, as examples of knowledge-creating companies. He writes that a beer can provided a Canon design team with the metaphoric inspiration they needed to design a reliable minicopier that boasts a disposable, cheap-to-produce photosensitive copier drum which is the source of 90 percent of all copier maintenance problems. Discussing their design problems over drinks one day, the task-force leader held up a beer can and wondered how much it cost to manufacture the aluminum can, which was similar in design to their ideal copier drum. By exploring how the drum was like and not like the beer can, the team came up with the technology to produce an aluminum copier drum at a low cost.

Suggested Reading

Nonaka, Ikujiro. "The Knowledge-Creating Company." *Harvard Business Review,* vol. 69, no. 6, November–December 1991, p. 96.

lateral thinking A set of attitudes, idioms, and techniques that can be used to cut across patterns in self-organizing systems. Created by Edward de Bono, lateral thinking is creative and discontinuous, as opposed to vertical thinking. Lateral thinking, he says, "turns up an idea; vertical thinking develops it."

Related Terms breakpoint, discontinuous change, knowledge-creating company, managerial frame, outside-the-box thinking, paradigm shift, paradox, six thinking hats, thunderbolt thinking, upside-down thinking

Examples

- When a company is attempting to promote innovation, lateral thinking techniques or exercises can be used to encourage creativity and break out of old patterns of perception. De Bono gives an example of executives being asked to think of product innovations for an old product line. By associating the sense of smell with this product, which had nothing in particular to do with the olfactory sense, executives were able to think of the product from a different perspective.

Suggested Reading

De Bono, Edward. *Serious Creativity: Using the Power of Lateral Thinking to Create New Ideas.* New York: HarperBusiness, 1992.

De Bono, Edward. *Lateral Thinking.* New York: Harper & Row, 1971.

McGartland, Grace. *Thunderbolt Thinking: Transform Your Insights & Options Into Powerful Business Results.* Austin, Texas: Bernard-Davis, 1994.

Van Oech, Roger. *A Whack on the Side of the Head.* New York: Warner, 1990.

lead management A management system that consistently inspires quality workmanship and production. Lead management is epitomized by the Japanese business dedication to quality management as developed by W. Edwards Deming.

Lead managers, as described by William Glasser, subscribe to a four-step system:

Step 1. They engage workers in an ongoing dialogue to promote quality work.

Step 2. The lead manager or a designee demonstrates (models) the job so that management's expectations are clear both for the product/service and for the worker's responsibility. According to Glasser (1994), this clarification of expectation helps increase the worker's sense of control over the production process.

Step 3. The role of inspectors is largely eliminated from the production process. Workers themselves become responsible for producing quality products.

Step 4.   A commitment to continuous improvement is made part
              of the work contract by both managers and workers.

See continuous improvement, empowerment, total quality management (TQM).

lean production model/lean manufacturing Characterized by centralized coordination and high-performance quality indicators. Lean production managers in both the service and manufacturing sectors are committed to reengineering their business processes to trim overhead and minimize inventory.

Under this model, permanent core knowledge workers form a production network that is usually separated from the low-paid outside peripheral or contingent workforce, which is housed in smaller business firms run by suppliers and subcontractors. By emphasizing flexible, contingent employment, commentators say that these firms are creating a dual labor market of wage inequality. These decentralized corporations do, however, have extraordinary networking capability and will, in the estimation of some management theorists, dominate the emerging global economy (Harrison, 1994).

Related Terms   accordion management, agile manufacturing, BPR, contingent workforce, flexible production, globalization, JIT, cost management

Examples
  • In their 1990 study of the changing economics of car design, Womack, Jones, and Ross use the term *lean manufacturing* to describe the manufacturing system pioneered by Toyota, one of many Japanese companies that employ the lean production model. By cutting inventory and using teams of workers to eliminate bottlenecks, the car company has cut its production time and improved quality over the last forty years.

Suggested Reading
    Harrison, Bennett. *Lean and Mean, the Changing Landscape of Corporate Power in the Age of Flexibility.* New York: Basic Books, 1994.
    Landvater, Darryl V. *Planning & Control in the Age of Lean Production.* Essex Junction, Vt.: Oliver Wight, 1994.
    Womack, J. P., D. T. Jones, and D. Ross. *The Machine That Changed the World.* New York: Rawson Associates, 1990.

learning organization A corporation or a noncorporation where acquisition of knowledge is a key to success. Peter Senge, Director of Systems Thinking and Organizational Learning at MIT's Sloan School of Management, has defined five disciplines that will characterize the learning organization of the future.

Systems thinking—the ability to see the connections and patterns within an organization

Personal mastery—the constant growth of individuals within a company

Mental models—an understanding of the assumptions and traditions that guide an organization. Knowing where the company is today can lead to what management gurus call paradigm shifts, an ability to deal with a dynamic business environment experiencing discontinuous change

Building shared vision—management's presentation of a vision of the future that guides and inspires the organization, allowing for corporate transformation

Team learning—the importance of team learning to the organization

Senge views these disciplines as developmental pathways for acquiring skills and competencies. He says that practicing these disciplines is different from emulating a specific model. Rather, the learning disciplines will converge and create not *the* learning organization but "a new wave of experimentation and advancement."

Senge describes systems thinking, which fosters the ability to see the connections between the self and the world, as the fifth discipline, which will unite these five practices and build an organization where "people are continually discovering how they create their reality."

Related Terms   collective learning, fifth discipline, fifth generation management, fourth generation management, industry foresight, intellectual capital, intelligent organization, managerial frame, paradigm shift, team learning

Examples

- In the organization of the future, Senge sees the "manager as researcher and designer." For example, in firms dedicated to the practice of total quality, managers will still be decision makers but they will also join with workers in the investigation and improvement of the work process.
- Senge compares the dynamic development of the learning organization to the convergence of technologies that created the DC-3. The DC-3 was not the end of the process but rather the commencement of the commercial airline industry.

Suggested Reading

Savage, Charles M., *Fifth Generation Management: Integration of Enterprises Through Human Networking.* Burlington, Mass.: Digital Press, 1990.

Senge, Peter M. *The Fifth Discipline: The Art and Practice of the Learning Organization.* New York: Doubleday, 1990.

lot sizes of one   *See* mass customization, segments of one.

loyalty-based management   Retaining customers and keeping them loyal to a corporation and its products and services. Coined by Frederick Reichheld, director of the loyalty practice at Bain. *See* customer franchise management.

management by decree (MBD)   Often the management style of choice when the chief executive and the board of directors are under extreme pressure from shareholders to improve performance and no longer have the patience for the participatory rituals of change management. Specific performance objectives and, even more important, the career-breaking consequences of failure are made clear in management edicts that receive hands-on attention from senior executives. MBD is most effective when a quick improvement in return on capital employed (after-tax profits divided by total capital employed) is imperative. The goal in these circumstances could range from reducing reliance on bank borrowing to improving operating profit by cutting expenses.

Related Terms   cost management, denominator management, downsizing, rightsizing

Examples
- A company worried that its banks may withdraw its credit lines may issue a management decree to executives to improve its cash position within forty-five days. This objective can be achieved by freeing up capital tied up in inventories, fixed assets, and receivables. Such quick-hit programs to reduce or avoid borrowing are frequently seen and often dramatically successful tactics during recessions.
- Why does management issue decrees? For the S&P industrials, cost cuts raised profits from 12.2 percent of sales in 1992 to 12.9 percent in 1993. Given investor expectation in 1994, economist and merchant banker John Rutledge calculated that each dollar cut from operating expenses could raise the equity value of a firm with a 40 percent tax rate by $10.20.

Suggested Reading
Hamel, Gary, and C. K. Prahalad. *Competing for the Future: Breakthrough Strategies for Seizing Control of Your Industry and Creating the Markets of Tomorrow.* Boston: Harvard Business School Press, 1994.
Rutledge, John. "Just Do It." *Forbes,* February 14, 1994, p. 142.

managerial frame   An intellectual or frame around which many managers cannot see. The combination of education and business experience creates this frame and affects the choice of technologies, sales channels, and competitive strategies and particularly senior management focus, among other perspectives. An inability to escape this management frame can limit a company's ability to innovate.

Related Terms industry foresight, knowledge-creating company, lateral thinking, mental model (learning organization), paradigm shift

Examples
- Until recently, the managerial frame at banks did not encourage thinking of consumer savers as investors.
- The concept of computers as portable and of operating systems as graphic interfaces was outside the managerial frame of much of the computer industry before the Macintosh was introduced.

Suggested Reading
De Bono, Edward. *Lateral Thinking.* New York: Harper & Row, 1971.
Hamel, Gary, and C. K. Prahalad. *Competing for the Future: Breakthrough Strategies for Seizing Control of Your Industry and Creating the Markets of Tomorrow.* Boston: Harvard business School Press, 1994.

market-driven management A discipline that advocates a value-oriented approach that goes beyond product/price/promotion/distribution marketing to pursue close and enduring relationships with customers. This strategy sees the sale as the beginning of a process and seeks to understand how the customer defines value whether it is in product quality, follow-up service, or anticipation of new technology requirements. Marketing has become a key component in the management strategy of the new corporate enterprise looking for growth.

In market-driven companies, marketing departments are often eliminated as stand-alone groups to cut overhead costs and to create stronger customer relationships. The marketing professionals become members of multidisciplinary teams focused on processes or customers.

Related Terms customer franchise, customer focus, mass customization, market segmentation, marketing excellent companies, maxi-marketing, relationship marketing, valufacture

Examples
- In 1994, the Amos Tuck School at Dartmouth College offered a week-long executive education course in market-driven management, which was positioned as "an entirely new way of thinking about the process of winning and retaining customers."
- The Rover Group makes it a practice to contact all buyers of Discovery, Defender, and Range Rover automobiles by telephone or mail to inquire about quality of customer service and product satisfaction.

Suggested Reading

Brady, John, and Ian Davis. "Marketing's Mid-life Crisis." *The McKinsey Quarterly*, no. 2, 1993.

Marketing at the Crossroads. Coopers & Lybrand, 43 Temple Road, Birmingham B2 5JT, England.

Summers, Diane. "Corporate Zits Beware." *The Financial Times*, April 14, 1994, p. 9.

mass customization   The ability to make individually customized and high-quality goods at the low cost of standardized, mass-produced products.

Stan Davis coined the term as the new paradigm of management, a shift from the mass production of standardized goods that built American industry. B. Joseph Pine uses the term as a category for companies that successfully implement mass customization and build "organic" production systems. These dynamic networks are composed of relatively autonomous operating units and include the loosely defined jobs typical of highly skilled craftspeople. Governed by an adaptable structure, the company can reconfigure technology, processes, and units quickly and efficiently to give the individual consumer exactly what is ordered.

Related Terms   continuous improvement, customer-centered organization, customer franchise management, diversified quality, informationalize, organic organization, product extensions, segments of one

Examples

- By early 1992, Toyota Motor Company was offering customers a wide range of product options and could manufacture and deliver a made-to-order car within three days. While the number of options has since decreased, customer direct access/self-design systems still allow Toyota to offer customized cars based on the buyer's individual specifications.
- Bally Engineering Structures, Inc. of Bally, Pennsylvania, made a strategic decision to change from a company that offered specific products, such as refrigerated rooms and walk-in coolers, to become a mass customizer offering a wider range of these products tailored to individual customer needs. Organized in flexible teams, employees are connected via an electronic computer network that allows sales representatives to design each refrigerator product in the customer's office on a laptop computer and transmit the order via modem to the factory floor. An integrated software module specifies the process modules—manufacturing units such as floors, ceilings, or refrigeration units—that are required to fulfill the order.

- *Time* magazine now has the information technology that allows it to tailor magazine contents to reader preferences by geography and uses that information to maximize advertising revenues.

Suggested Reading
> Davis, Stan. *Future Perfect.* New York: Addison-Wesley, 1987.
> Pine, B. Joseph, II. *Mass Customization: The New Frontier in Business Competition.* Boston: Harvard Business School Press, 1993.

maxi-marketing   Forging personalized bonds that both tie into and build social networks based on product consumption. Marketing consultants Stan Rapp and Thomas Collins have written several books exploring the shift from mass marketing to such individualized marketing. Along the way they coined the buzzword *maxi-marketing.* As a method of developing long-term relationships with customers, maxi-marketing forges personalized bonds that both tie into and build social networks based on product consumption.

Related Terms   channels management, customer-centered organization, customer franchise management, loyalty-based management, mass customization, organic organization, segments of one

Examples
- In France, Nestle baby food has positioned itself as a company that customers rely on for many aspects of their children's health and well-being. Throughout the summer months, Nestle operates rest stops along the main French roads to assist vacationers traveling with small children. These centers have become genuine social gathering places for young families, serving 600,000 baby meals during 120,000 roadside visits during the summer of 1993. As a result of this maxi-marketing strategy, Nestle's market share for its baby food division has gained twenty percentage points since 1985.

Suggested Reading
> Rapp, Stan, and Thomas L. Collins. *Beyond Maxi-Marketing: The New Power of Caring and Daring.* New York: McGraw-Hill, 1994.
> Rapp, Stan, and Thomas L. Collins. "The New Marketing: Sell and Socialize." *The New York Times,* February 20, 1994, p. III.

MBD   *See* management by decree.

mental model   *See* learning organization, managerial frame.

middle-up-down management   A management style characteristic of Japanese companies. Identified and given a name by Ikujiro Nonaka, a Tokyo professor, this buzzword described the interactive roles played by all layers of management in a company. Middle managers who are close both to the customer base and to technological change may be the source of innovative ideas that they send both up and down the organization scalar. Senior managers recognize this bottom-up participation and act as coaches to promote organizational learning and flexibility.

This management style contrasts to the typical Western corporate hierarchy that can set management against staff. Charles Hampden-Turner and Fons Trompenaars describe middle-up-down structures as similar to a nested Chinese puzzle box.

Related Terms   bottom-up participation, empowerment

Examples

- In Japanese companies, senior managers play the role of coordinators rather than leaders, acknowledging the hands-on contribution and experiences of lower-level employees.

Suggested Reading

Hampden-Turner, Charles, and Fons Trompenaars. *The Seven Cultures of Capitalism.* New York: Doubleday, 1994.

mission statement   *See* vision/visioning.

molecular organization   *See* change management, virtual corporation.

new-age leadership   *See* fourth generation management, fifth generation management, post-heroic leadership, servant leadership, stewardship, virtual leadership.

new motivators   Management gurus who speak at corporate seminars and social events. *See* Chapter 2: Behind the Buzzwords: The Gurus of Change Management.

numerator management   An executive commitment to regenerating a company and its industry to achieve ambitious, long-term, profitable growth. The statistics used to measure performance—ROI, ROA, ROCE, among others—have two components, a numerator (net income) and a denominator (usually assets, equity, or investment). Growth strategies concentrate on improving net income or figures in the numerator. Gary Hamel and C. K. Prahalad call this management strategy numerator management. *See* core competencies, corporate transformation, denominator management, EVA, organizational architecture.

OLÉ   Acronym describing a system where production workers who would otherwise be idle or laid off during periods of slack demand are crosstrained to produce other products ancillary to the traditional line of business. Off-line employment, or Olé, is the proposal of Sidney Harman, Chairman of Harman International industries Inc. and former Commerce Under Secretary, who is known as a visionary espousing a new labor-management culture. Olé offers an internal labor buffer to promote employee loyalty, retain skilled workers, increase job security, and create a culture of long-term employment. Olé is an alternative to downsizing the workforce and then adding contingency workers during upswings.

Related Terms   contingent workforce, core workforce, flexible management, lean production model

Examples
- Harman International employs approximately 1,500 production workers in the San Fernando Valley. During downturns, this $665 million consumer-electronic company shifts its workers to producing clock faces using scrap wood from speaker cabinets. Harman is committed to a training rotation program that reduces its need for outsourcing and brings this work back inside the plant for company employees to produce.

Suggested Reading
Kuttner, Robert. "Talking Marriage and Thinking One-Night Stand." *Business Week*, October 18, 1993, p. 16.

on-demand hyperlearning   *See* kanbrain.

on-line market   *See* social computing.

open-ended management   *See* horizontal corporation.

opportunity   Buzzword associated with growth and competition. Opportunity as an adjective is applied to many aspects of a company's future competitiveness. For example,

Opportunity Arena—The future areas where a firm builds the necessary core competencies so that it can become an industry leader.

Opportunity Horizon—The vista of future market opportunities or, as Gary Hamel and C. K. Prahalad say, the ability to see the bird in the bush.

Opportunity Share—In contrast to market share, opportunity share is competition for dominance in markets that either do not yet exist or are just emerging.

These and other opportunity buzzwords are used by Gary Hamel and C. K. Prahalad in their writings. *See* Hamel and Prahalad (1994) in the Selected Bibliography.

organizational architecture   Addresses corporate organization from the point of view of how work, people, and both formal and informal structures fit together. The result of such organizational rethinking is frequently an emphasis on internal alliances and autonomous work teams.

David Nadler defines organizational architecture as the art of shaping behavioral space and discusses it on three levels: the architecture of business or work units, the architecture of enterprises, and the architecture of interenterprise relations.

Related Terms   autonomous work teams, completeness, congruence model of effectiveness, high-performance workplace, shamrock organization, teamnets

Examples

- The term *organizational architecture* first gained national prominence as a change management buzzword when David Nadler worked on the reorganization of Xerox in 1991/92. The team that helped design the new structure created a new organization where profit and loss responsibility was moved out of the executive office and down to business team general managers. The resulting organization chart showed corporate staff at the bottom supporting business teams and districts at the top.
- Nadler describes the philosophical framework for his own consulting firm, Delta Consulting, as the "congruence model of effectiveness" to encapsulate how the key elements of the organization fit together.
- Using architectural metaphors with inventiveness and insight, Robert Tomasko has written a business book that examines the problem of developing the best organizational structure that fits each company's unique requirements.

Suggested Reading

Byrne, John. "Management's New Gurus." *Business Week*, August 31, 1992, pp. 44–52.

Kearns, David T., and David A. Nadler. *Prophets in the Dark: How Xerox Reinvented Itself and Beat Back the Japanese*. New York: Harper-Business, 1992.

Nadler, David A., Mark S. Gerstein, Robert B. Shaw and Associates. *Organizational Architecture: Designing for Changing Organizations*. San Francisco: Jossey-Bass, 1992.

Tomasko, Robert M. *Rethinking the Corporation: The Architecture of Change*. New York: AMACOM, 1993.

outside-the-box thinking   *See* breakpoint, industry foresight, lateral thinking, managerial frame, paradigm shift, thunderbolt thinking.

outsourcing Describes the purchase of peripheral services from outside vendors or sources. These services, such as data processing or payroll processing, are usually regarded as noncore products, although they may support the core product. Outsourcing can add value to a corporation by cutting staff overhead costs while increasing efficiency by taking advantage of the economics of scale and focus.

Related Terms activity value analysis, contingent workforce, core products, insourcing, lean production model, partnering, shamrock organization

Examples
- Many banks have begun to oursource their back office data processing function as a way to reduce overhead. By purchasing these services from a top-of-the-line supplier, the banks can concentrate on their core businesses of providing innovative financial service products while obtaining the use of state-of-the-art technology without the capital investment. In one case, J. P. Morgan outsources the back office processing of its American Depository Receipt business to an outside supplier.
- Outsourcing pension fund management to insurance companies has become a standard practice for corporate America. For example, firms such as Prudential and Massachusetts Mutual provide 401K fund management to their clients.

Suggested Reading
Keyes, Jessica. *Infotrends: The Competitive Use of Information.* New York: McGraw-Hill, 1993.
Laabs, Jennifer. "Successful Outsourcing Depends on Critical Factors." *Personnel Journal,* vol. 72, no. 10, October 1993, pp. 51–56.

overhead value analysis (OVA) *See* activity-value analysis.

pals (pooling, allying, and linking companies) Buzzword acronym invented by Rosabeth Moss Kanter to describe independent companies that choose to work together for their mutually competitive advantage. *See* alliance, federalism, globalization, partnering partnerships.

paradigm shift A fundamental change in a major aspect of a business situation or marketplace. This new way of looking at something may be caused by innovations in technology, science, or any other factor influencing a situation. Thomas Kuhn coined the term in 1962. Don Tapscott and Art Caston believe that four paradigm shifts are impacting business in the decade of the 1990s: the new technology (user-centered network computing), a new geopolitical order (a volatile, multipolar world), the new enterprise (the open, networked organization), and the new business environment (a competitive, dynamic marketplace).

Related Terms   breakpoint, discontinuous change, lateral thinking, managerial frame, thunderbolt thinking, upside down thinking

Examples
- The bulldozing of the Berlin Wall in the late 1980s caused a paradigm shift in the political order that broke through the hostilities of the Cold War Era and opened up the markets of Eastern Europe to the West.
- The introduction of electronic spreadsheets such as Lotus 1-2-3 that could be used with personal computers precipitated a paradigm shift in the world of banking where what-if risk scenarios could suddenly be recalculated in moments instead of hours.

Suggested Reading

Barker, Joel Arthur. *Paradigms: The Business of Discovering the Future.* New York: HarperBusiness, 1993.

Kuhn, Thomas. *The Structure of Scientific Revolutions*, 2nd ed. Chicago: University of Chicago Press, 1970.

Naisbitt, John. *Global Paradox: The Bigger the World Economy, the More Powerful Its Smallest Players.* New York: Morrow, 1994.

Popcorn, Faith. *The Popcorn Report.* New York: HarperBusiness, 1992.

Tapscott, Don, and Art Caston. *Paradigm Shift: The New Promise of Information Technology.* New York: McGraw-Hill, 1993.

participative management   An open, nonsecretive approach to management where every employee has a say, although not a democratic vote, in the decision-making process as well as a right to understand the results. Max DePree describes the most effective contemporary management process as participative management, which is based on respect for the individual and an understanding that each individual has the right to participate regardless of hierarchical standing. *See* followership, empowerment.

partnering/partnerships   The development of long-term relationships that can, for example, bring customer and supplier closer together, recognize and draw from each other's area of expertise, and build manufacturing networks based on human capital. In contrast to adversarial relationships where corporations leverage their way to success by negotiating their suppliers into submission, destroying competitors, or acquiring companies for their human or financial assets, partnering strategies look beyond the short-term price objective of cutting costs.

  The trust generated by this strategy can allow a smooth transition into the next generation of products and, according to Patricia Moody, create a collective enterprise advantage. For a successful customer-supplier network to work, Moody says it should include a commitment to seven drivers: superior quality, timeliness, excellent communications, flexibility, an attitude of continuous improvement, the habit of collaboration, and trust.

Related Terms   alliance, continuous improvement, JIT (just-in-time production), information partnerships, *keiretsu*, outsourcing, teamnets

Examples

- United Airlines has developed numerous noncash alliances with other carriers including Lufthansa in Europe, allowing it to expand overseas routes and cut costs.
- An information partnership between Chrysler and its suppliers has been able to speed up the auto company's product development cycle and cut expenses. Suppliers now receive electronic access to over 6,000 active engineering standards that used to require over 80,000 printed pages.
- Walmart and Sears have both developed partnerships with suppliers, allowing them to sell a wide variety of products at highly competitive market prices.
- The networks of equipment suppliers, venture capitalists, lawyers, and inventors in Silicon Valley enterprises provide an example of a new, evolving form of partnership.

Suggested Reading

Hanan, Mack. *Growth Partnering: How to Build Your Company's Profits by Building Customer Profits.* New York: AMACOM, 1992.

Moody, Patricia E. *Breakthrough Partnering: Creating a Collective Enterprise Advantage.* Essex Junction, Vt.: Oliver Wight, 1993.

passengers   *See* road kill.

pay for performance   Compensation system, also called performance-related pay (PRP). Base salaries in PRP systems usually remain in a steady state with minimal increases linked to inflation, and significant increases in pay come in the form of performance-related bonuses, paid either yearly or following completion of a project. Such programs, which gained popularity in the high growth years of the 1980s, feature large rewards for significant contributions to the company's bottom line. A significant portion of CEO and other senior executive compensation is usually linked to company performance often in the form of stock options or deferred compensation where payout it tied to length of services.

Performance compensation systems are one way to build employee loyalty and retain key personnel.

Recently, managers have expressed dissatisfaction with performance-related compensation systems citing a number of problems: salaries tend to flex upward, poor performers are disincented to improve their performance, definitions of good performance are hard to arrive at, and even "winners" appear to have short-term memories and are encouraged only briefly and may leave after bonuses are paid.

Related Terms   gainsharing, performance-related gift (PRG)

Examples

- Fluor Corp. has asked customers to provide input to their pay for performance system. Fluor's chairman has persuaded some clients to give a quarterly report card rating for Fluor project teams using a scale of 1 to 10 on performance measures such as scheduling, safety, and cost. In contrast to man-hour contracts, these Fluor teams are now paid 50 percent of the incentive fee if the score is 5 and 100 percent if the score is 10.
- The Los Angeles freeway reconstruction was completed in record time following a recent earthquake. The construction company was told it would be paid on a performance basis; it would be fined for failing to meet the agreed-upon deadline and paid a bonus for each day earlier that the construction was completed.
- In Japan, companies show their appreciation for noteworthy performance with foreign holidays to Hawaii and golf club memberships.
- When Avon Products, the American direct-sales beauty products company, tried to change its incentive system the "Avon ladies" rebelled. The company had tried to insist that instead of trading points accumulated for good performance for gifts, these bonus points could only be used to buy savings bonds. Faced with an angry and hostile sales force, the company immediately introduced a streamlined, upgraded sales incentive program with a new catalogue of gifts.
- GTE pays money managers based on their results. Managers who surpass their investment benchmarks by 5 percent can double their fees. Those who fail can get only a fraction of their usual fee.

Suggested Reading

"Giving It Away." *The Economist,* April 23, 1994, p. 11.

Liesse, Julie. "Pay for Performance Picking Up Speed." *Advertising Age,* vol. 64, no. 33, August 9, 1993, pp. 19–20.

Patten, Thomas H., Jr. *Pay: Employee Compensation and Incentive Plans.* New York: Free Press, 1977.

Tanner, L.D. "Seeking a Pay Formula." *Monthly Labor Review,* vol. 115, no. 3, March 1992, pp. 41–42.

performance engineering™   A customer-driven, whole-system perspective toward changing performance at three critical levels—process reengineering, organization transformation, and business reinvention. The framework presents a practical way to position a company for sustained profitable growth and enhanced market value.

Related Terms BPR (business process reengineering), business reinvention, organization transformation, process reengineering, reengineering

Examples

- Fred Adair, who leads Mercer Management Consulting's Performance Engineering™ practice, cites the example of an electric utility where teams of company employees reengineered seven business processes: high bill inquiry, budgeting, transmission systems planning, service restoration, materials management, generation maintenance, and telecommunications planning. The benefits from reengineering these processes included a reduction in the total cost of the high bill inquiry process, a decrease in call volume, and a drop in related cycle time. Outage frequency was also reduced.

Suggested Reading

Hammer, Michael, and James Champy. *Reengineering the Corporation: A Manifesto for Business Revolution.* New York: HarperCollins, 1993.

post-heroic leadership A term popularized by Jim Huey of *Fortune* magazine to describe the new style of leadership needed in the information-age corporation. The characteristics of a post-heroic leader are self-awareness, a passion for personal growth, commitment to skills building, and conceptual awareness. The post-heroic leader demonstrates excellent communications skills and an ability to inspire an empowered workforce of individuals.

Related Terms empowerment, leadership industry, new age leadership, servant leadership, stewardship, virtual leadership

Examples

- The concept may be new, but nominees for the post-heroic leadership hall of fame are already being noted. Among them are Levi Straus executive Robert Haas, Herman Miller chairman Max DePree, Wilbert L. "Bill" Gore, founder of W. L. Gore Associates.

Suggested Reading

Bass, Bernard M. *Stogdill's Handbook of Leadership: A Survey of Theory and Research.* New York: Free Press, 1981.

Conger, Jay A. *The Charismatic Leader: Behind the Mystique of Exceptional Leadership.* San Francisco: Jossey-Bass Publishers, 1989.

DePree, Max. *Leadership Jazz.* New York: Dell, 1992.

DePree, Max. *Leadership Is an Art.* New York: Dell, 1990.

McGregor, Douglas. *The Human Side of Enterprise.* New York: Mc-Graw-Hill, 1960.

PRG (performance-related gift)   Presents from the corporation to a valued employee as an alternative to the cash bonuses in pay-for-performance systems. The gifts, which may range from Caribbean cruises to color television sets and golf club memberships, are a tangible, ongoing reminder of a job well done and the firm's appreciation. *See* pay for performance.

process reengineering   *See* BPR, performance engineering™, reengineering.

quality management   *See* total quality management (TQM).

reengineering   Fundamentally redesigning core processes to make them more efficient and sensitive to customer needs. Often associated with across-the-board cost cutting, the best reengineering projects take a unified approach to improving a company's operating efficiency at the same time that they strive to enhance revenues.

Reengineering, which may be undertaken to improve profitability and enhance a corporation's market value, should involve staff at all levels of a company, from senior management to clerical workers. Job design and organizational structures will be overhauled, and work will be organized around the outcome and not the task itself.

Failure to take a radical approach to reengineering can result in mediocre results and a slow return to traditional approaches for doing business.

Well-run, collaborative reengineering projects, in contrast, restructure a company and empower employees. The transformation of a corporation's culture can instill a new sense of competitiveness and customer service as well as an ongoing awareness of the need to contain costs. Employees learn to approach every job, as one money center bank officer told us, with the goal of doing it "faster-better-cheaper-quicker."

Popularized although not invented by Michael Hammer and James Champy, who offered a "manifesto" for a "business revolution," reengineering goes under many names, and every consultant and management guru has their own system for achieving it. The subject of numerous books ranging from the philosophical treatise to hands-on instruction guides, reengineering is a benchmark topic of all change management theory and practice.

Related Terms   business process reengineering (BPR), change management, corporate transformation, declutter, downsizing, organizational architecture, performance engineering™, reinvention, reshaping, restructuring, rightsizing

Examples

- Fluor Corp. successfully reengineered its mining and metals unit so that the engineering and construction services giant saw its engineering projects grow 230 percent from $300 million to over $1 billion with only a 25 percent increase in the workforce. Before the reorganization, each local office maintained its own teams of engineering, marketing, and operations managers that operated autonomously. Today, a mobile management team connected through an electronic work-sharing network cooperates on global projects no matter what their actual physical location.
- Star Bank Corporation of Ohio undertook a restructuring project in 1993 with the goal of improving the bank's ratio of costs to revenues, decreasing it from 63 percent to 55 percent. According to Oliver W. Waddell, then chairman, president, and CEO, the project, named EXCEL, "redesigned and reengineered Star's businesses." EXCEL improved customer service by eliminating management tiers and placing decision making closer to the marketplace.
- ITT Sheraton Corp. reengineered its hotel chain in 1992 with the aid of Michael Hammer. By reengineering processes and eliminating unnecessary paperwork, Sheraton was able to cut staff in a typical 300-room hotel from 40 managers and 200 employees to 14 managers and 140 employees while still maintaining high customer satisfaction.
- A 1993 survey of senior executive representing the Fortune 1000 companies by a major consulting firm revealed that approximately half were likely to engage an outside firm to assist in a reengineering project within a year. In the survey, 88 percent of those companies undertaking a reengineering effort said that they expected it would tighten the alignment between their processes and customer values.

Suggested Reading

Adair, Fred. "Reengineering: Fad or Future." *The Edge: Wharton Consulting Journal.* March 1994, pp. 102–104.

Allen, Paul. *Reengineering the Bank.* Chicago: Probus, 1994.

Byrne, John. "Management's New Gurus." *Business Week,* August 31, 1992, pp. 44–52.

Hammer, Michael, and James Champy. *Reengineering the Corporation: A Manifesto for Business Revolution.* New York: HarperBusiness, 1993.

Manganelli, Raymond, and Mark M. Klein. *The Reengineering Handbook.* New York: AMACOM, 1994.

reinventing the corporation   A signature phrase of John Naisbitt that describes the ability of a corporation to change and grow. *See* corporate transformation.

renewal factor   A signature phrase of Robert Waterman, Jr., that describes the ability of an organization to reinvent itself. *See* corporate transformation.

reshape, resize   Signature phrases of Robert Tomasko that describe the process of corporate change. *See* corporate transformation, downsizing, reengineering, rightsizing.

restructuring   *See* BPR, organizational architecture, reengineering, strategic architecture.

return on management (ROM)   A value-added concept, developed by Paul Strassmann, a former Xerox executive. ROM calculates the productivity ratio of a management structure. The ratio is useful in reengineering or restructuring exercises. ROM is analogous to Return on Investment (ROI). The formula is:

$$ROM = \frac{\text{Management Value Added}}{\text{Management Costs}}$$

In this calculation, management value added is the difference between the total value a company adds (the difference between total sale price plus production costs) and the portion of that value that includes a company's operating expenses (labor plus capital expenditures). Management costs are labor costs, management tools such as personal computers, and services that managers purchase, such as consultants and travel.

Note: This use of ROM should not be confused with the computer acronym, which stands for read only memory.

Related Terms   deaveraged profitability, EVA, shareholder value

Examples

• Strassmann calculated that the total ROM for American industry is low, about 1.2, and draws the conclusion that most American managers are being paid more than what they deliver in value-added terms. He says that companies with the highest ROM display the least amount of vertical integration, outsourcing more services and cutting their overhead.

Suggested Reading

The Strategic Planning Institute. *Management Productivity and Information Technology.* Cambridge, Mass.: The Strategic Planning Institute, 1983.

reversal theory   Suggests career horizons can be broadened and employee performance improved if individuals learn to reverse attitudes toward types of work and become motivationally versatile. Most people can, according to this theory, learn to change or reverse their standard motivational approach with training.

Upheavals in the world of work have called into doubt traditional progress up the career ladder within one company or even in one industry or profession. In such an atmosphere of distrust, managers face the issue of how to motivate employees and retain their wholehearted dedication. Although many psychologists have claimed that motivation is a basic and virtually unchangeable part of human personality, new research into changing work patterns has produced reversal theory and suggested new approaches to behavior modification.

Related Terms   demassing, career design, career path

Examples

- Managers at an industrial plant who are asked to affect an across-the-board cost cut of 15 percent may find the prospect of laying off long-term employees extremely disturbing both from the viewpoint of personal stress and the negative response from the local community. With training, the managers can be taught to focus on the ultimate negatives of not accomplishing the cost cut, such as reduced profitability, a consequent drop in equity valuation, and loss of the company's credit rating, all of which could lead to closing of the plant, which would have far greater negative impact on the surrounding community and their personal careers.

Suggested Reading

Apter, Michael. *Reversal Theory—Motivation, Emotion and Personality.* New York: Routledge, 1989.

reverse engineering   To evaluate competitors' strengths and compare them with their own, corporations will conduct a reverse engineering exercise, reducing product or services to the fundamental or core products that add value. This term, which can be compared to factoring a mathematics equation, is also applied in strategic benchmarking when competitor's business strategies are analyzed. *See* benchmarking, best practices.

rightsizing   Making a company the "right size for its industry and markets to ensure profitability." A restructuring company that evaluates tasks to identify duplications and inefficiencies and to create a disciplined approach to pricing before it lays off workers or sells ancillary product lines is said to be getting to its right size.

Some critics say that rightsizing is a euphemism for downsizing because it always seems to involve cutting staff. Others would say it is an example of activity value analysis.

Related Terms   activity value analysis (AVA), downsizing, reductions-in-force, reengineering, restructuring

Examples

- Paul Allen, the Chairman of Aston Limited Partners, says that rightsizing protects against a decrease in customer service or the loss of revenues often caused by the arbitrary cost cutting characteristic of downsizing exercises which do not differentiate between fat and muscle. At the banks Aston has restructured, including Chase Lincoln, CoreStates, and Star Banc Corporation, they have unbundled the services offered to customers as part of the rightsizing exercise. The goal is to deliver greater profitability to the corporation by ensuring that bank services are priced consistently with perceived customer value and price increases meeting with minimal customer resistance.

Suggested Reading
Allen, Paul. *Reengineering the Bank.* Chicago: Probus, 1994.

road kill   Image for companies that fail to anticipate the future of their industries and are, like small animals at the roadside, mowed down by the competition. Extending this metaphor, Gary Hamel and C. K. Prahalad describe companies that successfully reinvent their industries and earn the highest profits as "drivers," whereas companies that get carried along and whose profits are only modest are called "passengers." *See* Hamel and Prahalad (1994) in Selected Bibliography.

scenario planning   A what-if technique for projecting developments in fluid political and economic situations. Scenario planning takes into account and interprets cultural traits, economic factors, and political events.

Related Terms   long-range planning, what-if analysis

Examples

- The Royal Dutch/Shell Group used scenario planning in 1984 to predict that the rise of Mikhail Gorbachev would bring widespread changes to the former Soviet Union.

Suggested Reading
Fischer, A.B., A.H. Moore, et al. "Is Long-Range Planning Worth It?" *Fortune,* vol. 12, no. 9, April 23, 1993, pp. 281–283.
Schwartz, Peter. *The Art of the Long View.* New York: Doubleday, 1991.

Yergin, Daniel, and Thane Gustafson. *Russia 2010: And What It Means for the World*. New York: Random House, 1994.

s-curve analysis   Describes the timing for developing a new product or service in relationship to the return on investment. When a product life cycle is plotted on a graph where the x-axis is funds invested and the y-axis represents performance, the shape that usually appears is a sigmoid curve, a sinuous line shaped like an S, which starts low, rises steeply and falls off sharply. To maintain its competitive edge, a company must invest in a new product or strategy before the peak of the curve when the current winner will go into decline.

Related Terms   breakpoint, informationalize, innovation, lateral thinking, managerial frame, paradigm shift, second curve, sigmoid curve, staying ahead of the curve, thunderbolt thinking

Examples

- In his book *Innovation,* Richard Foster applies s-curve analysis to the dynamics of technology management. He contends that companies either abandon new technologies too quickly or hold on to older ones too long because management does not understand the curve on which technology develops, first slowly, then extremely rapidly, and finally slowly in its maturity. Foster contends that successful companies are "attackers" who recognize the economics of substitution and are willing to cannibalize current products when they may appear to be most lucrative to begin the cycle of renewal and innovation again.
- An example of Foster's analysis of technology is evident in National Cash Register's failure to incorporate electronic technology into its products in the late 1960s. By May 1971 the company was forced to announce that $140 million of new cash registers were impossible to sell and would be written off because they could not compete with the cheaper, easier-to-use electronic machines entering the market.
- Microsoft Corporation, the largest software company in the world, has repeatedly moved quickly to upgrade its Windows operating system, well before the s-curve reaches its peak. New features in the operating system spur users to upgrade and pave the way for new versions of word processing and graphics software programs that can then take advantage of these capabilities.
- In an attempt to escape the rapidly declining s-curve for credit cards, financial services companies are focusing on niches, slicing up the marketplace. Chase Manhattan Bank, for example, issued nine new cards during the 1993–1994 year, attempting to stop erosion of its overall market share. American Express is in the process

of issuing several credit and charge cards with a variety of fee structures.

- The television redefined home entertainment, impacting both films and radio. The interactive capabilities offered by the home computer may be doing the same to network and cable TV, as well as consumer banking.

Suggested Reading

Foster, Richard. *Innovation: The Attacker's Advantage*. New York: Summit Books, 1986.

Handy, Charles. *The Age of Paradox*. Boston: Harvard University Press, 1994.

segments of one   Single, low-cost but high-quality customized products made possible by information technology. Serving these market segments of one calls for a flexible and modular corporate organization structure that can both listen to a customer's needs, produce, and deliver a profitable product.

Related Terms   continuous improvement, customer franchise management, informationalize, lot sizes of one, mass customization

Examples

- Greeting card stores now have the information technology that allows customers to create and print out personalized greeting cards.
- Music stores allow listeners to engineer their own personal choice compact discs by picking songs from a variety of artists.

Suggested Reading

Moody, Patricia E. *Breakthrough Partnering: Creating a Collective Enterprise Advantage*. Essex Junction, Vt.: Oliver Wight, 1993.

Pine, B. Joseph, II, Bart Victor, and Earl W. Sasser, Jr. "Making Mass Customization Work." *Harvard Business Review*, September–October, 1990, pp. 105–111.

Pine, B. Joseph, II. *Mass Customization: The New Frontier in Business Competition*, Boston: Harvard Business School Press, 1993.

self-directed work teams   *See* teams.

self-leadership   *See* empowerment.

self-managed work teams   *See* teams.

servant leadership   Empowering people with ideas and information rather than directly telling them what to do. The challenge for today's business leaders, according to Karl Albrecht, is "to create meaning" through servant leadership. Under this new leadership model, executives will be visionaries who encourage a customer focus. As team-builders these leaders will promote an ethic of performance and cooperation, becoming living symbols of the success premise of the enterprise. Finally, these leaders will be buck-stoppers who can make the tough decisions and take responsibility.

Related Terms   new age leadership, post-heroic leadership, stewardship

Examples
- James Cayne, CEO of Bear Stearns, says that he always acts as if he is "running for mayor," an example of servant leadership.

Suggested Reading

Albrecht, Karl. *The Northbound Train: Finding the Purpose, Setting the Direction, Shaping the Destiny of Your Organization.* New York, AMACOM, 1994.

Greenleaf, Robert. *Servant Leadership.* Mahwah, N.J.: Paulist Press, 1977.

Kiechel, W., III. "The Leader as Servant." *Fortune*, vol. 125, no. 9, May 4, 1992, pp. 121–122.

shamrock organization   Representation of the three different groups of workers who make up the information-age corporation and their three, vastly different sets of expectations for compensation and benefits, management, and organization. Used by Charles Handy.

One leaf of the shamrock or segment of the new organization represents the core workforce which includes managers, technicians, and qualified professionals. This group owns the knowledge that distinguishes a company from its competitors, and there are individuals bound to the organization both with "hoops of gold," as Handy describes the salary packages, and expectations for flexible, committed performance.

The second leaf of the shamrock represents organizations outside the company to whom work is contracted. These are nonessential workers or units that can be replaced without damage to a company's unique competitive standing, such as data processing operations, cleaning services that maintain buildings, and suppliers of raw materials or even parts in a manufacturing process.

The third leaf of the shamrock is the temporary or part-time, flexible labor force of just-in-time employees, the fastest growing segment of the workforce.

Related Terms   contingency workforce, horizontal corporation, lean production model, olé, organizational architecture, outsourcing, virtual corporation

Examples
- Xerox Corporation has awarded a ten-year contract to Electronic Data Systems (EDS) to run its global telecommunications and com-

puter networks, an example of the second leaf of the shamrock organization.

Suggested Reading
> Handy, Charles. *The Age of Unreason.* Boston: Harvard University Press, 1989.

shareholder value analysis (SVA)   A framework for judging business performance in terms of the financial gain to shareholders, introduced by Alfred Rappaport in the mid-1980s. Rappaport promoted, updated, and institutionalized this process, particularly for the evaluation of acquisitions. He eschewed traditional accounting standards for judging the success of American corporations and promotes use of numbers such as annual sales and growth of earnings.

Rappaport's system sets out new applications for the shareholder value approach and new ways of measuring whether corporate strategy actually creates economic value for shareholders. He offers a step-by-step approach to acquisition analysis and developed a computer model (Alcar) used by many corporate finance specialists.

Lines of business (LOBs), for example, are analyzed by employing risk-adjusted discounted cash flows. LOBs must exceed the threshold rate of return to be considered value creators for shareholders. Those LOBs that do not reach hurdle rates are classed as value destroyers. Combining the economics for an LOB with a strategic analysis of both the LOB and the overall company helps management classify units as core, transitional, exit, or appropriate for sale.

Related Terms   deaveraged profitability, economic value analysis (EVA) earnings per share (EPS), return on equity (ROE), return on assets (ROA), return on management (ROM), value creator, value destroyer

Examples
- Shareholder value has become a primary means of evaluating not only a company's performance but also its leadership. Rappaport gives Citicorp's performance under Walter Wriston as an example of this method of evaluating leadership performance. Although Citicorp's returns to shareholders during Wriston's 1970–1984 tenure were almost identical to the return on the S&P 500 index, Citicorp shareholders did better than shareholders of other large U.S. banks—approximately 50 percent better than shareholders of Bank of America, Manufacturers Hanover, and Chemical Bank and almost 100 percent better than Chase Manhattan Bank shareholders.
- Michael A. Miles, chairman and chief executive officer of Philip Morris Co., resigned in 1994 following a struggle with the board over plans to split the company into separate food and tobacco

businesses. The split had been advocated by big shareholders who saw the move as a way to raise the company's depressed stockmarket value.

- Lotus Development Corp.'s shares fell 28 percent ($14.375) during one day of trading in mid-1994 as investors reacted to the disclosure that second quarter results would be disappointing, decreasing shareholder value. The company reportedly said that per-share earnings would be approximately half of most estimates and that sales would also fall short of analysts' projections partly because of delays in key products.
- The sale of its retail branch network and exit from consumer banking allowed Bankers Trust to concentrate on the institutional side of its business and resulted in a substantial increase in value for shareholders.
- News that Microsoft Corporation would be shipping prerelease test versions of its Chicago upgrade to Windows in June 1994 sent the company's stock price up 50 cents in a down market. The market recognized the long-term potential for expanded software sales that would follow launch of the new operating program in 1995.
- According to a 1994 Mercer Management Consulting study, profitable growth has the greatest impact on a company's shareholder value, outpacing cost cutting and other initiatives.

Suggested Reading

Rappaport, Alfred. *Creating Shareholder Value: The New Standard for Business Performance.* New York: Free Press, 1986.

Wendel, Charles B. "Four Sharp Tools for Learning How Your Bank Measures Up." *American Banker,* September 27, 1993, pp. 18–19.

Wenner, David, and Richard W. LeBer. "Managing for Shareholder Value—From Top to Bottom." *Harvard Business Review,* November–December 1989, pp. 52–66.

six thinking hats   System invented by management guru Edward de Bono that he promotes as a fundamental change in the basis of Western thought. Appears to be an extension of de Bono's concept of lateral thinking.

De Bono's system identifies six states of mind or "thought processes" that can be used in the analysis of any issue. During training sessions, he asks participants "to wear" real hats of different colors to teach them how to shift gears and think as a group or team. Colors of these thinking hats correspond to the following thought processes:

White hat:	Information gathering
Red hat:	Feelings and emotions

Black hat:	Caution, criticism
Yellow hat:	Benefits and feasibility studies
Green hat:	New ideas
Blue hat:	A metahat that unites the entire thinking process

Eventually, individuals trained in the thinking hat technique can put on an imagined hat to shift perspective and explore thoughts and ideas that might otherwise have been repressed by the logical systems derived from Socrates, Plato, and Aristotle.

Related Terms   breakpoint, industry foresight, lateral thinking, managerial frame, paradigm shift

Examples
- IBM, Federal Express, Du Pont, and the Mormon Church all reportedly have been trained in de Bono's thinking process.
- *The Financial Times* reports that at Marzotto in Italy, there are "thinking hat" posters throughout the company's buildings and that at Prudential in Canada, hats have been woven into the carpets.

Suggested Reading
De Bono, Edward. *Six Thinking Hats.* Boston: Little, Brown, 1985.
Kellaway, Lucy. "Put on your thinking caps." *The Financial Times,* June 17, 1994, p. 10.

social architecture   Warren Bennis's signature phrase for corporate culture.

social computing   An extension of the idea that computer networks and easy-to-use software will put on-line computing into the hands of consumers. Social computing is a marketing management concept that says the connection between large companies and their customers will be increasingly defined by on-line computer technology for the sales and distribution of products and other communications.

Related Terms   channels management, information superhighway, informationalize, Internet, on-line market, virtual marketplace, wired company

Examples
- Home banking or advertising on Prodigy is an example of social computing.
- Small merchants are finding that the Internet is a new channel for distribution. It offers the potential of a "storefront in cyberspace." According to *The New York Times,* Grant's Flowers and Greenhouses in Ann Arbor, Michigan, for example, has found that it is receiving as many orders through the Internet, including one from

Japan, as it does through FTD Mercury, the electronic system that links florists worldwide.

* The success of *Wired* magazine, a monthly publication that deals with the issues associated with on-line commercial and social relationships, is testimony to the growing spread of social computing.

Suggested Reading

Lewis, Peter H. "Getting Down to Business on the Net." *The New York Times*, Sunday, June 19, 1994, pp. 3–1, 3–6.

Wired, a monthly publication of Wired USA Ltd., 544 Second Street, San Francisco, Calif. 94107–1427.

spin-off   Focused, streamlined companies separated from larger corporate structures. Also known as *carve-outs* and *split-offs*.

spin-outs   When a company seeks to promote innovation, it may stake entrepreneurs to a new enterprise in which the parent company retains some equity. *See* bunsha, intrapreneuring.

stewardship   Described by Peter Block, who developed the model of stewardship as it applies to the business world, as an "alternative to leadership." He emphasizes the element of service at the core of this discipline, yet he draws a distinction between accountability, which is a key factor in stewardship, and the implicit desire for control inherent in the concept of leadership.

According to Block, stewardship does not dictate behavior but "gives us the guidance system for navigating [the] intersection of governance, spirituality, and the marketplace." For business organizations to change and survive, he sees three strong business issues that a governance strategy based on stewardship must address in the postindustrial marketplace now taking shape. These issues are doing more with less, learning to adapt to customers and our marketplace, and creating passion and commitment among employees.

The system that Block proposes for redesigning the workplace incorporates many ideas found in other discussions of the new business enterprise. However, he takes these theories a step further into what he calls the realm of "political reform" by viewing the business enterprise as a social system and advocating a redistribution of power and wealth. His specific proposals for reform in the compensation system, human resource management, budgetary and financial practices, and management practices provide a model for a more democratic and economically successful organization where spirituality and ethics are strongly held values.

Related Terms   empowerment, followership post-heroic leadership, servant leadership, theory Z, virtual leadership

Examples
- Lou Gerstner, chairman of IBM, has been described by *The New York Times* as fulfilling a stewardship role for the computer giant during its recovery phase of the mid-1990s.

Suggested Reading
> *At Work: Stories of Tomorrow's Workplace,* a Newsletter of Stewardship Ideas in Action. San Francisco: Berrett-Koehler Publishers, Item no. 19925-042.
> Block, Peter. *Stewardship: Choosing Service Over Self-Interest.* San Francisco: Berrett-Koehler Publishers, 1993.

strategic architecture   Buzzword that presents the concept of a corporatewide strategy that provides the architecture for action and planning. Used by C. K. Prahalad and Gary Hamel to describe the road map of the future for a corporate enterprise. The strategic architecture or long-term plan for development of the corporation will:
- Identify core competencies and establishes objectives for building them and the resulting core products
- Provide a logic for end product development, resource allocation, staff recruitment, and market focus

Related Terms   core competencies, core products, end products, industry foresight, intellectual leadership, market focus, opportunity horizon, organizational architecture, vision

Examples
- In the mid-1980s, Vickers, a supplier of hydraulic components such as pumps and valves to the defense, aerospace, earth moving, and automotive markets, developed a strategic architecture. The plan, which grew out of a realization that unless the company developed new skills, it would not be able to protect traditional markets or take advantage of developing opportunities, was based on a ten- to fifteen-year time horizon. Anticipated changes in technology were placed in the context of the core competencies that would be needed to meet emerging customer needs. The strategic architecture was not a specific forecast of end products, services, or even technologies. But it did provide a guide for competence development and a basis for making acquisitions, recruiting staff, building alliances, and establishing end product development priorities as well as market focus.

Suggested Reading
> Hamel, Gary, and C. K. Prahalad. *Competing for the Future: Breakthrough Strategies for Seizing Control of Your Industry and Creating the Markets of Tomorrow.* Boston: Harvard Business School Press, 1994.

Nadler, David A., Mark S. Gerstein, Robert B. Shaw and Associates. *Organizational Architecture: Designing for Changing Organizations.* San Francisco: Jossey-Bass, 1992.

sur/petition   Coined by management guru Edward de Bono to define a third phase of competition where integrated values combine to differentiate products and services. De Bono defines sur/petition as "seeking above" in contrast to competition, which means "seeking together" (de Bono, 1993). Companies that engage in sur/petition are what Michael Porter defined as "first movers," who choose to run their own race and work to create value monopolies that set themselves apart from mass producers.

Related Terms   first mover, gazelle, informationalize, mass customization, value chain, value monopolies, valufacture

Examples
- NVR, a company which works on behalf of an insurance policyholder to facilitate the sale of his or her life insurance policies, provides an example of sur/petition in the viatical industry which itself is an example of value added in the life insurance industry. Typically, viatical companies negotiate directly with life insurance policyholders to pay living benefits in anticipation of an early death. By acting as a representative of policyholders who face serious financial need due to life-threatening illnesses such as AIDS, NVR adds value by shopping the market for the best cash return to the seller and charging all fees to the buyer of the policy.
- When Chemical Bank's Middle Market Group invites the children of priority customers to attend a baseball clinic taught by the New York Mets, it is an example of sur/petition.

Suggested Reading
De Bono, Edward. *Sur/Petition: Creating Value Monopolies When Everyone Else Is Merely Competing.* New York: Harper Business, 1993.

symbolic managers   *See* post-heroic leadership.

systems thinking   *See* learning organization.

teams   Organizational groups, often project-based, that are a means to an end. In descriptions of the new corporate enterprise, the word manager is frequently replaced by team leader or project head, and the concept of teams, groups of individuals who are mutually accountable and committed to a common purpose for either the short term or the long term, has come to dominate discussions of effective organizations.

Teams—small numbers of people with complementary skills

working together toward a common purpose—can be both creative and an extremely practical, bottom-line-oriented way of doing business.

In a *Fortune* magazine article, Brian Dumaine defined five species of teams:

- *Management Teams.* This type of team draws its membership from managers of various functions who coordinate workflow among teams.
- *Problem-Solving Teams.* The knowledge workers who are members of these teams gather together to solve specific problems and then disband.
- *Quality Circles.* These are groups of workers and supervisors who meet regularly to tackle workplace problems and may be in danger of extinction.
- *Virtual Teams.* Under this new type of work team, workers communicate by computer and take turns at leadership.
- *Work Teams.* Empowered work teams are self-managed. They handle daily work.

Based on interviews with managers at companies such as Textron, NYNEX, Boeing, and Allina, Dumaine also put together some rules of engagement for teams:

- Use the right team for the right job.
- Create a hierarchy of teams.
- Trust the team to do its job.
- Tackle the people issues head-on.

Related Terms   adhocracy, autonomous work teams, buckyborgs, collective leadership, cross-functional teams, high-performance workplace, teaming, teamnets, teamwork, membership (as defined in the writings of Charles Handy), trust factor, work groups

Examples
- At Chrysler, new product teams have designed winning vehicles on a low, virtually shoestring budget.
- At Volvo's plant in Uddevalla, Sweden, individual teams are responsible for the assembly of entire cars and even have direct contact with customers.
- A benchmark study of 3M by a major consulting firm has shown that the company reduced its new product development cycle by 50 percent through teaming.
- A survey of Fortune 1000 companies showed that although 68 percent of these companies use self-managed or high-performance teams, only 10 percent of the workforce is organized in such teams.

Suggested Reading

Dumaine, Brian. "The Trouble With Teams." *Fortune,* vol. 130, no. 5, September 5, 1994, pp. 86–92.

Harrington-Mackin, Deborah. *The Team Building Tool Kit: Tips, Tactics, and Rules for Effective Workplace Teams.* New York: AMACOM, 1994.

"Information Technology Special Report: Managing in a Wired Company." *Fortune,* vol. 130, no. 1, July 11, 1994.

Katzenbach, Jon R., and Douglas K. Smith. *The Wisdom of Teams: Creating a High-Performance Organization.* Boston: Harvard Business School Press, 1993.

team learning   *See* learning organization, team.

teamnet   *See* co-opetition, horizontal corporation, *kaizen,* teams, virtual corporation.

Theory Z   Description of a culturally driven egalitarian organization that believes in collective responsibility. These companies are team oriented, do not foster a star system, and, as might be expected, are usually homogeneous. William G. Ouchi, who coined the buzzword and wrote the bestseller, identified the Theory Z style of management after extensive comparisons of American and Japanese management styles and their vastly different impact on productivity. Japanese productivity, he notes, increased at 400 percent the rate of productivity improvements in the United States during the post–World War II years.

Ouchi decided that productivity is "a problem of managerial organization" and that management skill rather than technology, investment, inflation, or regulation gives Japan its competitive advantage over the United States. He argues that to increase productivity, American corporations must foster a relationship of greater trust and intimacy between worker and manager, a relationship unhindered by bureaucratic constraints imposed either by the corporation or by external forces such as unions.

Ouchi presented thirteen steps for a company seeking to change from a bureaucratic to a participative organization. He estimated that a preliminary transition could be completed within two years but a full-scale change-over would take from ten to fifteen years to permeate every level of the organization.

Related Terms   empowerment, participative management, stewardship, teams, total quality management (TQM), trust factor

Examples

- Ouchi gives many functional examples of Theory Z Japanese companies as well as American companies that have made or are making the transition. Named at the top of his list are technology companies such as Hewlett-Packard and Intel. He also cites the transition plan pursued at General Motors for change at the plant level.

Suggested Reading
> Ouchi, William G. *Theory Z: How American Business Can Meet the Japanese Challenge.* New York: Avon Books, 1982.

thirteen steps   *See* Theory Z.

thunderbolt thinking   A buzzword coined by Grace McGartland to describe the sudden insights that can result in profitable business opportunities. *See* breakpoint, industry foresight, lateral thinking, paradigm shift, s-curve analysis.

time-based competition   The idea that time, like money, quality, and innovation, is a source of competitive advantage for every process found within an organization. George Stalk, Jr., of Boston Consulting elevated time management to the corporate level when he popularized the term time-based competition in the mid-1980s. Stalk urges companies to use speed to gain a competitive edge and to watch "cycle times" of processes such as product development.

Related Terms   cycle times, cycle-time reduction, hyperfast product development, hypercompetition, time-compression management

Examples
- Hertz's #1 Club Gold program not only offers extremely fast service to frequent customers but also helps focus employee attention on the customers who are most valuable to the company's bottom line. For example, drivers of Hertz buses at airports immediately ask boarding passengers to identify themselves as Gold Club members to ensure that their cars are ready upon arrival at the pick-up center where #1 Club customers can read an electronic bulletin board to find their rental car location.
- Taiwan companies are known for their ability to bring a product to market in ninety days or fewer, from concept to production.

Suggested Reading
> Stalk Jr., George. "Time—The Next Source of Competitive Advantage." *Harvard Business Review,* July–August, 1988, pp. 41–51.
> Stalk, Jr., George, and Thomas M. Hout. *Competing Against Time: How Time-Based Competition Is Reshaping Global Markets.* New York: Free Press, 1990.

time-compression management   *See* time-based competition.

total customer satisfaction (TCS)   *See* customer satisfaction.

total quality management (TQM)   The concept of quality products produced by totally committed and empowered workers and sold for a premium price. Many people associate the current popularity of total quality management as a management system with postwar Japan. However, the theory, perhaps as old as commerce itself, was articulated by Bell Labs in the 1920s and was central to the American World War II effort. The Americans taught it to the Japanese during the postwar occupation, and the Japanese, in turn, reintroduced TQM to the world in the 1970s.

Companies that successfully embrace TQM regard it as a four-part program based on a management/worker partnership to:

- Change the organization's culture to a team-driven environment.
- Train all employees in statistical process control (SPC) and other basic tools.
- Expand the reward system to recognize both team players and risk takers.
- Make the customer the center of all activity.

The quantification and positioning of this capitalistic approach to the marketplace took on a revivalist fervor in the 1980s. TQM has spawned, as might be expected, highly articulate, emotional critics and disciples.

The management gurus, led by W. Edwards Deming, Joseph Juran, and Philip Crosby, position quality management as a salvation strategy for the postindustrial corporation. Any disenchantment with TQM has, even the critics agree, resulted at least partly from incomplete implementations of the integrated program required to change a companywide culture.

Related Terms completeness, empowerment, high-performance workplace, partnership, quality circle, theory Z, zero defections

Examples
- Motorola, Federal Express, and Xerox are examples of companies that have embraced the TQM philosophy and succeeded. At Motorola, for example, a dedication to customer satisfaction is at the center of all product development, sales, and service. The result is the world's tiniest cellular phone and a planned global network of communications satellites.
- On the other side of the coin, McDonnell Douglas is often cited as a failure of TQM. Shortly after training 8,000 workers in two-week TQM seminars, the program stalled because cutbacks in the defense industry mandated extensive layoffs.
- Rochester Institute of Technology (RIT) and *USA Today* are sponsors of The Quality Cup. The award is inspired by "the power of the Quality movement" to revolutionize the way the United States does business.

- Nissan has created a training program at its Tennessee plant for its American suppliers. They attend a sixteen-day course on topics that range from W. Edwards Deming's quality management techniques to problem solving.

Suggested Reading

Bennet, James. "Detroit Struggles to Learn Another Lesson From Japan." *The New York Times,* June 19, 1994, p. 5.

Creech, Bill. *The Five Pillars of TQM.* New York: Truman Talley Books Dutton, 1994.

Crosby, Philip B. *Quality Is Free: The Art of Making Quality Certain.* New York: McGraw-Hill, 1979.

Deming, W. Edwards. *Quality, Productivity and Competitive Position.* Cambridge, Mass.: MIT Press, 1982.

Fisher, Donald C. *Measuring Up to the Baldrige.* New York: AMACOM, 1994.

Flood, Robert L. *Beyond TQM.* New York: Wiley, 1993.

Juran, Joseph M. *Juran on Leadership for Quality: An Executive Handbook.* New York: Free Press, 1989.

Juran, Joseph M. *Juran on Planning for Quality.* New York: McGraw-Hill, 1988.

Sashkin, Marshall, and Kenneth J. Kiser. *Putting Total Quality Management to Work: What TM Means, How to Use It, & How to Sustain It Over the Long Run.* San Francisco: Berrett-Koehler, 1993.

triad power   Economic insight in the three major geoeconomic regions: Japan, Europe, and the United States. As early as 1985, management guru Kenichi Ohmae argued that to compete in the emerging global marketplace, players would need to become "insiders" in this triad. The status of "insider" would give corporations political insight, greater immunity from protectionism, and consumer expertise, including the ability to test local markets for product and price preferences with an understanding of the local cultural preferences. By developing a base in each of these three economic centers and exploiting what he terms insiderization, companies, Ohmae argued, would also be better able to achieve global profitability through economies of scale.

Related Terms   alliances, globalization, insiderization, partnering, partnerships

Examples

- During 1994, two of the largest reinsurance companies in the United States, General Re Corp. and Employers Reinsurance Corp., both attempted to form an alliance with Colonia Konzern, one of

Europe's largest reinsurers, with the goal of expanding their operations in the European marketplace.

- In 1994, Unum, the Portland, Maine, insurance company, obtained a license from the Japanese Ministry of Finance to operate in Japan's tightly regulated insurance market. Since 1992, Unum has had an alliance with Yasuda Fire and Marine Insurance Company, a leading short-term disability provider in the Japanese market, and Yasuda will now introduce Unum's long-term disability products.

Suggested Reading
Ohmae, Kenichi. *Triad Power: The Coming Shape of Global Competition.* New York: Free Press, 1985.

trust factor   Proposal by John O. Whitney that management reach out to employees, easing controls and delegating responsibilities, resulting in higher productivity and greater competitiveness. Management theorists have begun to focus on methods beyond the balance sheet for revitalizing corporate profits and creativity in a post-recessionary, slow-growth environment where the scars of downsizing are still fresh in employee memories.

The trust factor, which presents a concept that is not often mentioned in the same sentence as management strategy, is the lever recognized by Whitney, a professor of management and executive director of the W. Edwards Deming Center for Quality Management at Columbia Business School, to eliminate waste and liberate an organization's creative energy. As might be expected, Whitney's ideas are an outgrowth of the Deming philosophy.

William G. Ouchi also discusses "trust" as an essential characteristic of the highly productive corporate enterprises he profiles as Theory Z companies.

Recently, management journalists exploring the impact of information technology networks on the management skill set have begun to suggest that creating a climate of trust is a way to foster responsible use of information.

Related Terms   credibility, empowerment, empowering leadership, teams, Theory Z, total quality management, transformational leadership

Examples
- In the flat organizations being created through the use of information technology networks, people from many different departments will share the same database and create a web of relationships based on trust. "This implies a whole set of reliances that didn't exist before" (*Fortune*, July 11, 1994, p. 5), according to Jim Manzi, CEO, Lotus Development.

Suggested Reading
> Stewart, Thomas A. "Managing in a Wired Company." *Fortune,* vol. 130, no. 1, July 11, 1994, pp. 44–56.
> Whitney, John O. *The Trust Factor: Liberating Profits & Restoring Corporate Vitality.* New York: McGraw-Hill, 1993.

upside-down   Adjective applied to a number of innovative ideas; generally describes the radical changes in expectation that are taking place in corporate and personal life including upside-down marketing, upside-down society, upside-down thinking.

Related Terms   age of chaos, age of unreason, discontinuous change, lateral thinking, paradigm shift, thunderbolt thinking

Examples
- Upside-down marketing, a buzzword popularized by George Walther, encapsulates a recognized marketing strategy that current or former customers represent the best opportunity for new business.
- Charles Handy sees the changing patterns of work as having significant impact on the social and political fabric of life. Reframing the expectations for work will extend to government and day-to-day life in Handy's vision of the future, calling for "upside-down thinking" about professional roles, income, and education and creating an "upside-down society."

Suggested Reading
> Handy, Charles. *The Age of Unreason.* Boston: Harvard Business School Press, 1989.
> Walther, George R. *Upside-Down Marketing.* New York: McGraw-Hill, 1994.

value-based strategy   *See* EVA, value chain.

value chain   Describing the activities a company performs to design, produce, market, deliver, and support its product. In creator Michael Porter's words, "A firm's value chain and the way it performs individual activities are a reflection of its history, its strategy, its approach to implementing its strategy, and the underlying economics of the activities themselves."

To gain maximum information from this approach, value chain analysis should be conducted for key activities, subactivities, major customers, and competitors. Such an analysis also requires a frank assessment of the key leverage points for both current and future high performance.

Porter states that there are five generic categories of primary activities which the value chain can diagnose: inbound logistics, operations, outbound logistics, marketing and sales, customer service.

In their recent book on competition, Gary Hamel and C. K. Prahalad suggest that the value chain concept does not go far enough in providing management with a practical understanding of its business and in challenging company leadership to reconsider approaches and strategies that may have been successful in the past but that are doomed to failure in the future.

Related Terms channels management, core competencies, deaveraged profitability

Examples

- Different firms in the same industry will have different value chains. For example, many airlines fly to London, but Virgin Air has differentiated itself by focusing on how to make coach a "fun" experience while providing excellent service and value. The airline also includes limousine pickup and drop-off in their business class section.
- Peeling the onion behind the five generic categories of primary activities is a key benefit to gain from value-chain analysis. Mercedes, threatened by new luxury car competitors from Japan, analyzed their approach to the business and repositioned itself to maintain strong market share.
- Taiwan's manufacturers have been described as knowing their place in the value chain of global information technology. Although it is a country with no cheap labor, Taiwan does have a population of young engineers who work for one-third less the salary of their U.S. counterparts. As a result, the Taiwan economy falls midway between the low-end, labor-intensive countries, such as the People's Republic of China, and the top-end, high-technology economies of the United States and Japan.

Suggested Reading

DeRose, Louis J. *The Value Network: Integrating the Five Critical Processes That Create Customer Satisfaction.* New York: AMACOM, 1994.

Hamel, Gary, and C. K. Prahalad. *Competing for the Future: Breakthrough Strategies for Seizing Control of Your Industry and Creating the Markets of Tomorrow.* Boston: Harvard Business School Press, 1994.

Hanan, Mack, and Peter Karp. *Competing on Value.* New York: AMACOM, 1991.

Porter, Michael. *Competitive Advantage.* New York: Free Press, 1985.

value creator A line of business (LOB) that exceeds the threshold rate of return. Such a high-value LOB is usually considered essential to the identity of a company and key to long-term profits. *See* shareholder value analysis.

value destroyer   Lines of business that do not reach hurdle rates of return and are marked for exit strategies. These low value units may have attractiveness either to a new market entrant or to a competitor with a different product or market share configuration and may be considered candidates for profitable sale. If there is a dearth of buyers or sale is not feasible for strategic reasons, liquidation may be preferable when exiting the business. *See* shareholder value analysis.

value network   *See* customer satisfaction.

values   A generic buzzword describing positive corporate behavior. Corporate values can describe a broad range of goals from vision and ethics to strategy and economic return. *See* value chain, valufacture, vision.

valufacture   A term invented by Edward de Bono. Valufacture or value manufacture—"the deliberate process of creating values"—helps describe the way competitors are differentiating customized products in today's new marketplace. *See* mass customization, sur/petition.

virtual   Adjective meaning having the outward appearance of a traditional brick-and-mortar structure or a legal organization but having a different and usually more informal internal structure. Virtual is being applied to many concepts for organizations and individual roles. These variations appear to be derived from the term *virtual reality*, which was originally trademarked (now given up) by Jaron Zepel Lanier, a computer inventor, who developed the eye phones and data gloves that allow the physical experience of simulated worlds generated by computer software. *See* virtual corporation, virtual enterprise, virtual office, virtual leadership, virtual marketplace.

virtual corporation   One model for the new organization. Tom Peters calls the virtual corporation the "corporation as rolodex" (Peters, 1994). It has also been described as the de-organized, disembodied, borderless, and boundaryless organization. It has been associated with alliances, federations, partnerships. But, whatever name or adjective is used, the virtual corporation is an innovative business structure organized around a few core modules and key skills and supported by a network of independent suppliers with the objective of keeping overhead low and productivity high. The ability to satisfy the customer becomes the driving force behind this organizational architecture.

    Although true virtual corporations usually have very few employees, the concepts of outsourcing nonkey functions to a peripheral or contingent workforce and tailoring services around customer needs can be used by many companies and industries, large and small.

Related Terms   alliance, borderless organization, boundaryless organization, buckyborgs, federalism, horizontal corporation, lean production model, PAL, partnership, virtual enterprise, virtual leadership, virtual marketplace, wired company

Examples

- Without the brick-and-mortar structure of a physical building or the human presence of on-site staff, banks, as well as other service companies, are experimenting with virtual reality, a hybrid discipline of the new information-age technology, to deliver better customer service.

  Through the holographic transmission of images, the on-line interaction between the customer at the off-site location and the bank officer, who may be hundreds of miles away, creates an "as-if" or virtual bank in a rented office cubical. Construction costs are eliminated, overhead costs are cut, and staff productivity as well as perception of customer service improves.

  Virtual banks give customers, using smart cards with computer chips that store a wealth of account information, the opportunity to review a wide assortment of financial services regardless of originating locations and regardless of their personal location.

- Randy W. Kirk, the president of AC International, says that he jumped on the virtual corporation bandwagon in 1981. Although his company controlled packaging, marketing, advertising, and product development, it owned no production equipment and had no labor overhead. What seemed like a benefit, however, became a series of troublesome problems ranging from late shipments to suppliers going bankrupt. Over the intervening years, Kirk's dissatisfaction with using suppliers to outsource components grew. AC International has since eschewed the virtual corporation and embraced a vertical corporate structure taking ownership of production to gain control of quality, delivery, and cost, all factors which Kirk says translate into better customer service.

- Two Purdue University professors are using customized hardware and off-the-shelf, virtual-reality software to allow groups of managers to walk together through a virtual corporation where symbolic domains represent such functions as cash flow and manufacturing operations.

Suggested Reading

Davidow, William H., and Michael S. Malone. *The Virtual Corporation: Structuring and Revitalizing the Corporation for the 21st Century.* New York: HarperBusiness, 1992.

Jarillo, J. Carlos. *Strategic Networks: Creating the Borderless Organization.* Boston: Reed Elsevier Group, 1993.
Kirk, Randy W. "It's About Control." *Inc.,* August 1994, pp. 25–26.

virtual enterprise   Charles Savage's signature phrase for the new corporation. *See* virtual corporation.

virtual leadership   Keeping employees of the information-age corporation focused on goals for production, service, and profitability as the hierarchical structures of the old corporate enterprise dissolve. These leaders of companies wired by information technology exercise less direct authority over specific work projects than their predecessors. Instead, they act as leaders of an empowered, self-leading workforce and stand as symbolic sources of values and a corporate vision. *See* followership, post-heroic leadership.

virtual marketplace   *See* social computing.

virtual office   Preserving the functions of an office without the need for a bricks-and-mortar location through telecommunications technologies. This virtual office can exist because employees communicate with fellow workers, consultants, and customers from any place that has a telephone line, at any time of the day or night. *See* hoteling, teams.

vision/visioning   The process of evaluating the focus and activities of an institution and outlining the mission and values to ensure top level performance has become not only a formal part of strategic planning but also a standard for morale building and a basis for performance evaluation.

Related Terms   corporate aspirations, industry foresight, intellectual leadership, mission statement, organizational architecture, strategic architecture, values

Examples
- Avis has 150 "mission statements," but the most famous one is certainly "We try harder."
- At some companies, visioning takes place in the boardroom and is communicated downward. At other companies, every unit fashions its own vision. At Marriott, for example, every hotel writes its own statement, which is signed by all staff, including clerks, bellhops, and maids.
- AST Computer has run a full-page advertisement in *The Wall Street Journal* that is headlined: "It's our vision that allows us to continually see double." The text that follows describes AST as a company that "thrives on delivering value" and "customer satisfaction."

- Purists such as Hilmar Kopper, speaker of the managing board of Deutsche Bank, claim to have a strategy rather than a vision which Kopper says "often turns into an illusion."

Suggested Reading

Albrecht, Karl. *The Northbound Train: Finding the Purpose, Setting the Direction, Shaping the Destiny of Your Organization.* New York, AMACOM, 1994.

Collins, James, and Jerry L. Parras. *Built to Last: Successful Habits of Visionary Companies.* New York: HarperBusiness, 1994.

wallenda factor A Warren Bennis signature phrase for the leadership ability to look forward and take responsibility for actions. *See* industry foresight, intellectual leadership.

wild duck Buzzword referring to those innovative employees, usually hired from the outside, who have a fresh perspective on a company's management strategy, business, and customers. The term originated as IBM jargon when founder Thomas Watson retold Kierkegaard's tale of wild ducks becoming domesticated, growing so fat and lazy that they gave up flying south for the winter. Watson's warning was that companies had to renew themselves to remain competitive.

Related Terms corporate venturing, corporateur, intrapreneur

Examples:

- IBM itself became a prime example of a company that became a tame duck in a wild duck industry. As it grew fat and lazy, content with an impressive share of the mainframe market, IBM got passed over by the younger generation of computer jocks who headed west to Silicon Valley. The company, which had significant employee layoffs during 1993–1994, still reportedly hired over 1,000 professionals from the outside looking to regain the wild duck perspective.

Suggested Reading

McMenamin, Brigid. "What Kind of Wild Duck Are You?" *Forbes,* vol. 153, no. 6, March 14, 1994, pp. 126–127.

wired company Term describing businesses that use information technology to build electronic networks connecting all levels of employees to each other and to databases. Information that once flowed only up and down through vertical hierarchies is freed in these companies. As a result, work can be carried out through networks by ad hoc, cross-functional teams, and the company's structure begins to take on an informal shape that calls for new management, product development, and marketing techniques.

Related Terms   horizontal corporation, human networks, informated company, informationalize, teams, virtual leadership

Examples

- Hewlett-Packard is an example of a wired company. *Fortune* magazine reports that each month H-P's 97,000 employees exchange 20 million E-mail messages internally and send 70,000 outside the company.
- Marsh McLennan reports that information networks are transforming the insurance business. Policies that cover commercial risks such as ships and buildings can now be compiled for resale and distributed electronically, a process that now takes days rather than weeks.

Suggested Reading

"Information Technology Special Report: Managing in a Wired Company." *Fortune*, vol. 130, no. 1, July 11, 1994.

workflow analysis   Evaluating a business as a series of interactions between customers and performers within the organization.

Each transaction or loop of the workflow can be broken into subloops. Using software now coming into the market, processes can be charted and monitored during each stage and tabs kept on individual performance. According to users, workflow management helps empower employees, making them feel more responsible for the quality of the process and its ongoing improvement. As a side effect, workflow also builds trust with management as employees demonstrate their initiative and the positive impact on customer relations.

The objective of this analysis is to achieve customer satisfaction throughout the four steps of the sales process:

1. An offer to sell or buy a service or product.
2. A negotiation and agreement as to what constitutes success.
3. Performance of the specified service or sale of the product.
4. Acceptance by the customer.

Related Terms   co-opetition, partnering, social computing, value chain, wired company

Examples

- IBM's personal computer plant in Austin, Texas, began to employ workflow management in 1990 to gain better control of product quality and production. IBM reports that workflow helped it trim its workforce at the plant by over 50 percent, shrink the manufacturing cycle from seven and a half days to one and a half days and increase the range of products from nineteen to eighty-five.

Suggested Reading

> Hammer, Michael, and James Champy. *Reengineering the Corporation: A Manifesto for Business Revolution.* New York: HarperBusiness, 1993.

work group A collection of individuals which has no "shared work product" and no shared purpose, goal, or approach save the overall health and profitability of the company (Katzenbach and Smith, 1994). Jon Katzenbach and Douglas Smith, two McKinsey consultants who have done extensive work on "teams," differentiate between "work groups" and "teams." Work groups do not share mutual accountability, one of the key definitions of a team. They do, however, provide mutual support to help achieve individual goals.

Related Terms collective leadership, high-performance workplace, teams

Examples

- Katzenbach and Smith cite the top management groups at successful companies, such as JP Morgan and General Electric, as examples of work groups. Leadership and membership is determined by external hierarchy instead of internal need. As a group, the individuals support each other's performance and achievement of their own goals for the betterment of the company.

Suggested Reading

> Katzenbach, Jon, and Douglas K. Smith. "Teams at the Top." *The McKinsey Quarterly,* no. 1, 1994, pp. 71–79.

zero defections A business strategy that mobilizes the organization to keep every customer that can be profitably serviced satisfied and active. Frederick Reichheld, director of the loyalty practice at Bain, and W. Earl Sasser developed this buzzword for customer service management from "zero defects," the quality management buzzword applied to the manufacturing process. If companies build off TQM principles and reduce defections to as little as 5 percent of their customer base, Reichheld and Sasser argue that profitability can be boosted 25–85 percent.

Related Terms customer franchise management, customer fulfillment, customer-centered organization, customer satisfaction, mass customization, time-based competition, TQM, upside-down marketing

Examples

- Great-West Life Assurance has an incentive plan that encourages brokers to find customers that will stay with the company for a long period of time. A premium is paid to brokers that meet customer-retention targets.
- In the late 1980s, Phil Bressler, the co-owner of five Domino Pizza

stores in Maryland, calculated that regular customers would spend more than $5,000 over the life of a ten-year franchise contract. He made sure that every employee knew that number, driving home the value of customer service.

Suggested Reading

Magrath, Allan J. *How to Achieve Zero-Defect Marketing.* New York: AMACOM, 1993.

Reichheld, Frederick F., and W. Earl Sasser, Jr. "Zero Defections: Quality Comes to Services." *Harvard Business Review*, September–October 1990, pp. 105–111.

Selected Bibliography

Adair, Fred. "Reengineering: Fad or Future." *The Edge: Wharton Consulting Journal*, March 1994, pp. 102–104.

Albrecht, Karl. *The Northbound Train: Finding the Purpose, Setting the Direction, Shaping the Destiny of Your Organization.* New York: AMACOM, 1994.

Aley, James, and Vivian Brownstein. "Where to Find Fast Growth." *Fortune*, vol. 130, no. 5, September 5, 1994, p. 25.

Allen, Paul. *Reengineering the Bank.* Chicago: Probus, 1994.

Ansari, A., and B. Modarress. *Just-in-Time Purchasing.* New York: Free Press, 1990.

Applebaum, Eileen, and Rosemary Batt. *The New American Workplace.* Ithaca, N.Y.: ILR Press, 1994.

Apter, Michael. *Reversal Theory—Motivation, Emotion and Personality.* New York: Routledge, 1989.

Atkins, Robert G., and N. Andrew Cohen. "Sales Channel Management: The Power of Innovation at the Point of Customer Contact." *Mercer Management Journal*, no. 2, 1994, pp. 9–27.

At Work: Stories of Tomorrow's Workplace, a Newsletter of Stewardship Ideas in Action. San Francisco, Calif.: Berrett-Koehler Publishers, Inc. Item no. 19925-042.

Barker, Joel Arthur. *Paradigms: The Business of Discovering the Future.* New York: HarperBusiness, 1993.

Bass, Bernard M. *Stogdill's Handbook of Leadership: A Survey of Theory and Research.* New York: Free Press: 1981.

Beer, M., R. Eisenstat, and B. Spector. "Why Change Programs Don't Produce Change." *Harvard Business Review*, November–December 1990, pp. 158–166.

Bennet, James. "Detroit Struggles to Learn Another Lesson From Japan." *The New York Times*, June 19, 1994, p. 5.

Bennis, Warren. *An Invented Life: Reflections on Leadership and Change.* Reading, Mass.: Addison-Wesley, 1993.

———. *On Becoming a Leader.* Reading, Mass.: Addison-Wesley, 1990.

Bennis, Warren, with Burt Nanus. *Leaders: The Strategies of Taking Charge.* New York: Harper & Row, 1985.

Birch, David, Anne Haggerty, and William Parsons. *Corporate Almanac 1994.* Cambridge, Mass.: Cognetics Inc., 1994.

Bleeke, Joel, and David Ernst, eds. *Collaborating to Compete: Using Strategic Alliances and Acquisitions in the Global Marketplace.* New York: Wiley, 1993.

Block, Peter. *The Empowered Manager: Positive Political Skills at Work.* San Francisco: Jossey-Bass, 1987.

Block, Peter. *Stewardship: Choosing Service Over Self-Interest.* San Francisco: Berrett-Koehler Publishers, Inc. 1993.

Block, Zena, and Ian C. McMillan, *Corporate Venturing: Creating New Businesses Within the Firm.* Boston: Harvard Business School Press, 1993.

Blumenthal, Barbara, and Philippe C. Haspeslagh. "Toward a Definition of Corporate Transformation." *Sloan Management Review,* Spring 1994, pp. 101–106.

Bogan, Christopher, and M. English. *Benchmarking for Best Practices.* New York: McGraw-Hill, 1994.

"Bounding Gazelles." *The Economist,* May 28, 1994, p. 65.

Bowles, Jerry, and Joshua Hammond. *Beyond Quality: How 50 Winning Companies Use Continuous Improvement.* New York: Putnam, 1991.

Brady, John, and Ian Davis. "Marketing's Mid-Life Crisis." *The McKinsey Quarterly,* no. 2, 1993.

Brown, Tom. "Farewell to the Furious '80s." *Industry Week,* January 8, 1990, p. 59.

Buckley, Neil. "Baked Beans Across Europe." *The Financial Times,* April 14, 1994, p. 9.

Burke, David. *Biz Talk 1: American Business Slang & Jargon.* Los Angeles: Optima, 1993.

Byham, William C., and Jeff Cox. *Zapp! The Lightning of Empowerment.* New York: Fawcett Columbine, 1988.

Byrne, John A. "Management's New Gurus." *Business Week,* August 31, 1992, pp. 44–52.

Byrne, John A. "The Horizontal Corporation." *Business Week,* December 20, 1993, pp. 76–83.

Casti, John L. *Complexification.* New York: HarperCollins, 1994.

Castro, Janice. "Disposable Workers." *Time,* March 29, 1993, p. 42.

Change Management: An Overview of Current Initiatives. Report No. 1068-94-RR, The Conference Board Europe, Avenue Louise 207, Box 5, B-1050, Brussels, Belgium.

Clifford, Donald K., Jr., and Richard E. Cavanagh. *The Winning Performance: How America's High Growth Midsize Companies Succeed.* New York: Bantam Books, 1985.

Collins, James, and Jerry L. Parras. *Built to Last: Successful Habits of Visionary Companies.* New York: HarperBusiness, 1994.

Conger, Jay A. *The Charismatic Leader: Behind the Mystique of Exceptional Leadership.* San Francisco: Jossey-Bass Publishers, 1989.

Cooper, R., and R.S. Kaplan. "Measure Costs Right: Make the Right Decisions." *Harvard Business Review,* no. 5, September–October 1988, pp. 96–103.

Coopers & Lybrand. *Marketing at the Crossroads.* Birmingham, U.K.

Covey, Stephen R. *The 7 Habits of Highly Effective People.* New York: Fireside, 1990.

Covey, Stephen R., A. Roger Merrill, and Rebecca R. Merrill. *First Things First: To Live, To Love, To Learn, To Leave a Legacy.* New York: Simon & Schuster, 1994.

Creech, Bill. *The Five Pillars of TQM: How to Make Total Quality Management Work for You.* New York: Truman Talley Books/Dutton, 1994.

Crosby, Philip B. *Quality Is Free: The Art of Making Quality Certain.* New York: McGraw-Hill, 1979.

Crosby, Philip B. *Completeness: Quality for the 21st Century.* New York: Penguin Books, 1994.

D'Aveni, Richard A., with Robert Gunther. *Hypercompetition: Managing the Dynamics of Strategic Maneuvering.* New York: Free Press, 1994.

Davenport, Thomas H., Michael Hammer, Tauno J. Metsisto. "How Executives Can Shape Their Company's Information Systems." *Harvard Business Review,* no. 2, 1989, pp. 130–134.

Davidow, William H., and Michael S. Malone. *The Virtual Corporation: Structuring and Revitalizing the Corporation for the 21st Century.* New York: HarperBusiness, 1992.

Davis, Stan, and Bill Davidson. *2020 Vision: Transform Your Business Today to Succeed in Tomorrow's Economy.* New York: Simon & Schuster, 1991.

Deal, Terrence E., and Allan A. Kennedy. *Corporate Cultures: The Rites and Rituals of Corporate Life.* Reading, Mass.: Addison-Wesley, 1982.

De Bono, Edward. *Lateral Thinking for Management.* New York: Harper & Row, 1971.

———. *Atlas of Management Thinking.* London: Penguin Books, 1983.

———. *Six Thinking Hats.* Boston: Little Brown and Company, 1985.

———. *Serious Creativity: Using the Power of Lateral Thinking to Create New Ideas.* New York: HarperBusiness, 1992.

———. *Sur/Petition: Creating Value Monopolies When Everyone Else Is Merely Competing.* New York: HarperBusiness, 1992.

Deming, W. Edwards. *Quality, Productivity and Competitive Position.* Cambridge, Mass.: MIT Press, 1982.

DePree, Max. *Leadership Is an Art.* New York: Dell Publishing, 1989.

———. *Leadership Jazz.* New York: Dell Publishing, 1989.

DeRose, Louis J., *The Value Network: Integrating the Five Critical Processes That Create Customer Satisfaction.* New York: AMACOM, 1994.

Dobyns, Lloyd, and Clare Crawford-Mason. *Thinking About Quality, Progress, Wisdom, and the Deming Philosophy.* New York: Times Books, 1994.

Douthwaite, Richard. *The Growth Illusion: How Economic Growth Has Enriched the Few, Impoverished the Many, and Endangered the Planet.* Tulsa: Oak Books, 1993.

Drucker, Peter F. *Innovation and Entrepreneurship: Practice and Principles.* New York: Harper & Row, 1954.

———. *The Practice of Management: A Study of the Most Important Function in American Society.* New York: Harper & Row, 1954.

———. *The Age of Discontinuity.* New York: Harper & Row, 1969.

———. *Management: Tasks, Responsibilities, Practices.* New York: Harper & Row, 1973.

———. "The Coming of the New Organization." *Harvard Business Review,* January–February 1988, pp. 45–53.

———. *Managing for the Future: The 1990s and Beyond.* New York: Truman Talley Books: Dutton, 1992.

———. "A Turnaround Primer." *The Wall Street Journal,* February 2, 1993, p. A-14.

Dumaine, Brian. "The Trouble With Teams." *Fortune,* vol. 130, no. 5, September 5, 1994, pp. 86–92.

Eccles, Robert G., and Nitin Nohria with James D. Berkeley. *Beyond the Hype: Rediscovering the Essence of Management.* Boston: Harvard Business School Press, 1992.

Edmondson, Gail, Neil Gross, Patrick Oster. "Philips Needs Laser Speed." *Business Week,* June 6, 1994, pp. 46–47.

Fierman, Jaclyn. "The Contingency Work Force." *Fortune,* vol. 19, no. 1, January 24, 1994, pp. 30–36.

Fischer, A. B., A. H. Moore, et al. "Is Long-Range Planning Worth It?" *Fortune,* vol. 21, no. 9, April 23, 1990, pp. 281–283.

Fisher, Donald C. *Measuring Up to the Baldrige.* New York: AMACOM, 1994.

Flood, Robert L. *Beyond TQM.* New York: Wiley, 1993.

Foster, Richard. *Innovation: The Attacker's Advantage.* New York: Summit, 1986.

Furnham, Adrian. "Death by a Thousand New Fangled Buzzwords." *The Financial Times,* February 4, 1994.

Garvin, David A. "How the Baldrige Award Really Works." *Harvard Business Review,* November–December 1991, pp. 80–93.

Gayeski, Diane. *Corporate Communications Management: The Renaissance Communicator in Information-Age Organizations.* Boston: Focal Press, 1993.

"Giving It Away." *The Economist,* April 23, 1994, p. 11.

Glasser, William. *The Control Theory Manager: Combining the Theory of William Glasser With the Wisdom of W. Edwards Deming to Explain Both What Quality Is And What Lead Managers Do to Achieve It.* New York: HarperBusiness, 1994.

Grant, Linda. "New Jewel in the Crown." *U.S. News & World Report,* February 28, 1994.

Green, Sir Owen. "Cadbury Critique—Excerpts From the Pall Mall Lecture on UK Corporate Governance." *The Financial Times,* February 25, 1994.

Greenleaf, Robert. *Servant Leadership.* Mahwah, N.J.: Paulist Press, 1977.

Gunsch, Dawn. "Turning Office Space Into a Hotel." *Personnel Journal,* vol. 71, no. 11, November 1992, pp. 16–19.

Hamel, Gary, and C. K. Prahalad. "Strategic Intent." *Harvard Business Review,* vol. 67, no. 3, 1989, pp. 63–76.

———. "Corporate Imagination and Expeditionary Marketing." *Harvard Business Review,* July–August 1991, pp. 81–92.

———. *Competing for the Future: Breakthrough Strategies for Seizing Control of Your Industry and Creating the Markets of Tomorrow.* Boston: Harvard Business School Press, 1994.

Hammer, Michael, and James Champy. *Reengineering the Corporation: A Manifesto for Business Revolution.* New York: HarperBusiness, 1993.

Hampden-Turner, Charles, and Fons Trompenaars. *The Seven Cultures of Capitalism.* New York: Doubleday, 1984.

Hanan, Mack. *Growth Partnering: How to Build Your Company's Profits by Building Customer Profits.* New York: AMACOM, 1992.

Hanan, Mack, and Peter Karp. *Competing on Value.* New York: AMACOM, 1991.

———. *Customer Satisfaction: How to Maximize, Measure, and Market Your Company's "Ultimate Product."* New York: AMACOM, 1991.

Handy, Charles. *Gods of Management: The Changing Work of Organizations.* London: Pan Books Ltd., 1978.

———. *The Age of Unreason.* Boston: Harvard Business School Press, 1989.

———. *The Age of Paradox.* Boston: Harvard Business School Press, 1994.

Harrington-Mackin, Deborah. *The Team Building Tool Kit: Tips, Tactics, and Rules for Effective Workplace Teams.* New York: AMACOM, 1994.

Harrison, Bennett. *Lean and Mean: The Changing Landscape of Corporate Power in the Age of Flexibility.* New York: BasicBooks, 1994.

Heifetz, Michael. *Leading Change, Overcoming Chaos: A Seven Stage Process for Making Change Succeed in Your Organization.* Berkeley, Calif.: Ten-Speed Press, 1993.

Henkoff, Ronald. "Getting Beyond Downsizing." *Fortune,* vol. 129, no. 1, January 10, 1994, pp. 58–64.

Heygate, Richard. "Technophobes, Don't Run Away Just Yet." *The Wall Street Journal,* August 15, 1994, p. A-10.

Hindle, Tim, chief contributor; edited by Alistair D. Williamson. *Field Guide to Business Terms: A Glossary of Essential Tools and Concepts for Today's Manager*. Boston: Harvard Business School Press, 1993.

Imai, Masaaki. *Kaizen (Ky'zen): The Key to Japan's Competitive Success*. New York: McGraw-Hill, 1986.

"Information Technology Special Report: Managing in a Wired Company." *Fortune*, vol. 130, no. 1, July 11, 1994.

Jarillo, J. Carlos. *Strategic Networks: Creating the Borderless Organization*. Boston: Reed Elsevier Group, 1993.

Johansson, Henry J., Patrick McHugh, A. John Pendlebury, and William Wheeler III. *Business Process Reengineering: BreakPoint Strategies for Market Dominance*. New York: Wiley, 1993.

Johnson, Hazel J. *The Banking Keiretsu*. Chicago: Probus Publishing Company, 1993.

Joiner, Brian L. *Fourth Generation Management: The New Business Consciousness*. New York: McGraw-Hill, 1994.

Juran, Joseph. *Juran on Planning for Quality*. New York: McGraw-Hill, 1988.

Juran, Joseph M. *Juran on Leadership for Quality: An Executive Handbook*. New York: Free Press, 1989.

Kanter, Rosabeth Moss. *The Change Masters: Corporate Entrepreneurs at Work*. New York: Simon & Schuster, 1983.

———. "The New Managerial Work." *Harvard Business Review*, November–December 1989, pp. 85–92.

———. *When Giants Learn to Dance*. New York: Simon & Schuster, 1989.

———. "Collaborative Advantage: The Art of Alliances." *Harvard Business Review*, July–August 1994, pp. 96–108.

Kanter, Rosabeth Moss, Barry A. Stein, and Todd D. Jick. *The Challenge of Organizational Change: How Companies Experience It and Leaders Guide It*. New York: Free Press, 1992.

Kaplan, Robert S., and David P. Norton. "Putting the Balanced Scorecard to Work." *Harvard Business Review*, vol. 71, no. 5, September–October 1993, pp. 134–147.

Karmarkar, Uday. "Getting Control of Just-in-Time." *Harvard Business Review*, September–October 1989, pp. 122–131.

Katzenbach, Jon R., and Douglas K. Smith. *The Wisdom of Teams: Creating the High-Performance Organizaton*. Boston: Harvard Business School Press, 1993.

———. "Teams at the Top." *The McKinsey Quarterly*, no. 1, 1994, pp. 71–79.

Kearns, David T., and David A. Nadler. *Prophets in the Dark: How Xerox Reinvented Itself and Beat Back the Japanese*. New York: HarperBusiness, 1992.

Kellaway, Lucy. "Put on Your Thinking Caps." *The Financial Times*, June 17, 1994, p. 10.

Kelley, Robert E. "In Praise of Followers." *Harvard Business Review,* no. 6, November–December 1988, pp. 142–148.

———. *The Power of Followership: How to Create Leaders People Want and Followers Who Lead Themselves.* New York: Doubleday, 1992.

Kennedy, Carol. *Instant Management: The Best Ideas From the People Who Have Made a Difference in How We Manage.* New York: William Morrow, 1991.

Keyes, Jessica. *Info Trends: The Competitive Use of Information.* New York: McGraw-Hill, 1993.

Kiechel W., III, and M. Rosenthal. "The Leader as Servant." *Fortune,* vol. 125, no. 9, May 4, 1992, pp. 121–122.

Kirk, Randy W. "It's About Control." *Inc.,* August 1994, pp. 25–26.

Kotler, John P., and James L. Heskett. *Corporate Culture and Performance.* New York: The Free Press, 1992.

Kovacevic, Antonio, and Nicholas Majluf. "Six States of IT Strategic Management." *Sloan Management Review,* Summer 1993, pp. 77–87.

Kuttner, Robert. "Talking Marriage and Thinking One-Night Stand." *Business Week,* October 18, 1993, p. 16.

Laabs, Jennifer J. "Successful Outsourcing Depends on Critical Factors." *Personnel Journal,* vol. 72, no. 10, October 1993, pp. 51–57.

Landrum, Gene N. *Profiles of Genius: Thirteen Creative Men Who Changed the World.* Buffalo: Prometheus Books, 1993.

Landvater, Darryl V. *Planning & Control in the Age of Lean Production.* Essex Junction, Vt. Oliver Wight, 1994.

Lewis, Peter H. "Getting Down to Business on the Net." *The New York Times,* June 19, 1994, pp. 3–1, 3–6.

Liesse, Julie. "Pay for Performance Picking Up Speed." *Advertising Age,* vol. 64, no. 33, August 9, 1993, 19–21.

Lipnack, Jessica, and Jeffrey Stames. *The TeamNet Factor: Bringing the Power of Boundary Crossing Into the Heart of Your Business.* Essex Junction, Vt.: Oliver Wight, 1993.

Lohr, Steve. "On the Road With Chairman Lou." *The New York Times,* June 26, 1994, pp. 3–1, 3–6.

Lord, James A., ed. "Management's Field of Dreams." *Consultants News,* June 1994, p. 5.

Lorenz, Christopher. "Need to Keep the Change Machine Under Control." *The Financial Times,* August 27, 1993, p. 9.

———. "Why Shakespeare was Wrong About Names." *The Financial Times,* December 31, 1993, p. 8.

———. "A New Mindset for the Manager." *The Financial Times,* February 16, 1994, p. 19.

Manganelli, Raymond, and Mark M. Klein. *The Reengineering Handbook.* New York: AMACOM, 1994.

Magrath, Allan J. *How to Achieve Zero-Defect Marketing.* New York: AMA-COM, 1993.

Marketing at the Crossroads. Coopers & Lybrand, 43 Temple Road, Birmingham B2 5JT, England.

Marlowe, Dick. "Buzzwords Killing the Common Sense in Management." *The Daily Record,* Morris County, N.J., February 16, 1994.

McGartland, Grace. *Thunderbolt Thinking: Transform Your Insights & Options Into Powerful Business Results.* Austin: Bernard-Davis, 1994.

McGregor, Douglas. *The Human Side of Enterprise.* New York: McGraw-Hill, 1960.

McMenamin, Brigid. "What Kind of Wild Duck Are You?" *Forbes,* vol. 153, no. 6, March 14, 1994, pp. 126–127.

Miller, James B. *The Corporate Coach: How to Build a Team of Loyal Customers and Happy Employees.* New York: St. Martin's Press, 1993.

Miyashita, Kenichi, and David Russell. *Keiretsu: Inside the Hidden Japanese Conglomerates.* New York: McGraw-Hill, 1994.

Moody, Patricia E. *Breakthrough Partnering: Creating a Collective Enterprise Advantage.* Essex Junction, Vt.: Oliver Wight, 1993.

Morgan, Gareth. *Imaginization: The Art of Creative Management.* U.K.: Sage, 1993.

Morris, Daniel C., and Joel S. Brandon. *Reengineering Your Business.* New York: McGraw-Hill, 1992.

Nadler, David, Marc S. Gerstein, and Robert Shaw. *Organizational Architecture: Designing for Changing Organizations.* San Francisco: Jossey-Bass, 1992.

Naisbitt, John. *Reinventing the Corporation.* New York: Warner Books, 1985.

———. *Global Paradox: The Bigger the World Economy, the More Powerful Its Smallest Players.* New York: William Morrow, 1994.

Nolan, Richard, Alex J. Pollock, and James P. Ware. "Creating the 21st Century Organization." *Stage by Stage 8:4,* Lexington, Mass.: Nolan, Norton and Co., Fall 1988, p. 11.

———. "Toward the Design of Network Organizations." *Stage by Stage 9:1,* Lexington, Mass.: Nolan, Norton and Co., Fall 1988, pp. 1–12.

Nollen, Stanley D. *New Work Schedules in Practice: Managing Time in a Changing Society.* New York: Van Nostrand Reinhold, 1982.

Nonaka, Ikujiro. "The Knowledge Creating Company." *Harvard Business Review,* November–December 1991, pp. 96–104.

O'Guin, Michael. *A Complete Guide to Activity Based Accounting.* Englewood Cliffs, N.J.: Prentice-Hall, 1991.

Ohmae, Kenichi. *The Mind of the Strategist: Business Planning for Competitive Advantage.* New York: Penguin, 1982.

———. *Triad Power: The Coming Shape of Global Competition.* New York: Free Press, 1985.

————. *The Borderless World: Power and Strategy in the Global Marketplace*. New York: HarperCollins, 1990.

Ostrenga, Michael R., and Terrence R. Ozan, Robert D. McIlhattan, and Marcus D. Harwood. *The Ernst & Young Guide to Total Cost Management*. New York: Wiley, 1992.

Ouchi, William G. *Theory Z: How American Business Can Meet the Japanese Challenge*. New York: Avon, 1982

Patten, Thomas H., Jr. *Pay: Employee Compensation and Incentive Plans*. New York: Free Press, 1977.

Patton, Phil. "The Virtual Office Becomes Reality." *The New York Times*, October 28, 1993, p. C1.

Perelman, Lewis J. "Kanban to Kanbrain." *Forbes*, June 6, 1994, pp. 84–85.

Peters, Tom. *Thriving on Chaos: Handbook for a Management Revolution*. New York: Knopf, 1987.

————. *Liberation Management: Necessary Disorganization for the Nanosecond Nineties*. New York: Knopf, 1992.

————. *The Tom Peters Seminar: Crazy Times Call for Crazy Organizations*. New York: Vintage, 1994.

Pinchot, Gifford, III. *Intrapreneuring: Why You Don't Have to Leave the Corporation to Become an Entrepreneur*. New York: Harper & Row, 1985.

Pinchot, Gifford, and Elizabeth Pinchot. *The End of Bureaucracy & The Rise of the Intelligent Organization*. San Francisco: Berrett-Koehler Publishers, Inc., 1993.

Pine, B. Joseph, II. *Mass Customization: The New Frontier in Business Competition*. Boston: Harvard Business School Press, 1993.

Pine, B. Joseph, II., Bart Victor, and Andrew Boynton. "Making Mass Customization Work." *Harvard Business Review*, September–October 1993, pp. 108–119.

Poirer, Charles C., and William F. Houser. *Business Partnering for Continuous Improvement: How to Forge Enduring Alliances Among Employees, Suppliers and Customers*. San Francisco: Berrett-Koehler Publishers, Inc., 1993.

Popcorn, Faith. *The Popcorn Report*. New York: HarperBusiness, 1992.

Porter, Michael E. *Competitive Strategy: Techniques for Analyzing Industry and Competitors*. New York: Free Press, 1980.

————. *Competitive Advantage*. New York: Free Press, 1985.

————. "The Competitive Advantage of Nations." *Harvard Business Review*, March–April 1990, pp. 73–93.

Prahalad, C. K., and Gary Hamel. "The Core Competence of the Corporation." *Harvard Business Review*, vol. 68, no. 3, May–June 1990, pp. 79–91.

Rapp, Stan, and Thomas L. Collins. *Beyond Maxi-Marketing: The New Power of Caring and Daring*. New York: McGraw-Hill, 1994.

Rappaport, Alfred. *Creating Shareholder Value: The New Standard for Business Performance.* New York: Free Press, 1986.

Rebollo, Kathy. "Microsoft: Bill Gates' Baby Is on Top of the World. Can It Stay There?" *Business Week,* February 24, 1992, pp. 62–64.

Rehfeld, John E. *Alchemy of a Leader: Combing Western and Japanese Management Skills to Transform Your Company.* New York: Wiley, 1994.

Reichheld, Frederick F., and W. Earl Sasser, Jr. "Zero Defections: Quality Comes to Service." *Harvard Business Review,* September–October 1990, pp. 105–111.

Rigdon, Joan E. "Retooling Lives—Technology Gains Are Cutting Costs, and Jobs, in Services." *The Wall Street Journal,* February 24, 1994, p. 1.

Robert, Michel. *Strategy Pure & Simple: How Winning CEOs Outthink Their Competition.* New York: McGraw-Hill, 1993.

Rodgers, T. J., William Taylor, and Rick Foreman. *No Excuses Management: Proven Systems for Starting Fast, Growing Quickly, and Surviving Hard Times.* New York: Doubleday, 1992.

Roger, Ian. "The Inside Story of a Model Multinational." *The Financial Times,* June 27, 1994, p. 9.

Rose, Frederick. "Job-Cutting Medicine Fails to Remedy Productivity Ills at Many Companies." *The Wall Street Journal,* June 7, 1994, p. A2.

Rutledge, John. "Just Do It." *Forbes,* February 14, 1994, p. 142.

Sakai, Kuniyasu, and Hiroshi Sekiyama as told to David Russell. *Bunsha: Improving Your Business Through Company Division.* New York: Intercultural Group, 1985.

Sashkin, Marshall, and Kenneth J. Kiser. *Putting Total Quality Management to Work: What TQM Means, How to Use it, & How to Sustain it Over the Long Run.* San Francisco: Berrett-Koehler, 1993.

Savage, Charles M. *Fifth Generation Management: Integration of Enterprises Through Human Networking.* Cambridge, Mass.: Digital Press, 1990.

Schaaf, Dick, and Margaret Kaeter. *Business Speak—4,000 Business Terms, Buzzwords, Acronyms, and Technical Words: All You Need to Say to Get Ahead in Corporate America.* New York: Warner Books, 1994.

Schonberger, Richard. "Total Quality Management Cuts a Broad Swath Through Manufacturing and Beyond." *American Management Briefing: Managing a Dynamic Organization.* New York: AMA Membership Publications Division, 1993.

Schwartz, Peter. *The Art of the Long View.* New York: Doubleday, 1992.

Scott, Cynthia, and Dennis T. Jaffe. *Empowerment: A Practical Guide for Success.* Menlo Park, Calif.: Crisp Publications, 1991.

Semler, Ricardo. *Maverick: The Success Story Behind the World's Most Unusual Workplace.* New York: Warner Books, 1993.

Senge, Peter. *The Fifth Discipline: The Art and Practice of the Learning Organization.* New York: Doubleday, 1990.

Senge, Peter, Charlotte Roberts, Richard B. Ross, Bryan J. Smith, and Art Kleiner. *The Fifth Discipline Fieldbook: Strategies and Tools for Building a Learning Organization*. New York: Doubleday, 1994.

Slater, Robert. *The New GE: How Jack Welch Revived an American Institution*. Homewood, Ill.: Business One Irwin, 1993.

————. *Get Better or Get Beaten! 31 Leadership Secrets From GE's Jack Welch*. New York: Irwin Professional Publishing, 1994.

Spendolini, Michael J. *The Benchmarking Book*. New York: AMACOM, 1992.

Sprout, Alison L. "Moving into the Virtual Office." *Fortune*, May 2, 1990, p. 103.

Serwer, Andrew E. "Lessons from America's Fastest Growing Companies." *Fortune*, vol. 3., no. 2, August 8, 1994, pp. 42–60.

Stalk, George, Jr., "Time—The Next Source of Competitive Advantage." *Harvard Business Review*, July–August 1988, pp. 41–51.

Stalk, George, Jr., and Thomas Hout. *Competing Against Time: How Time-Based Competition Is Reshaping Global Markets*. New York: Free Press, 1990.

Strategic Planning Institute. *Management Productivity and Information Technology*. Cambridge, Mass.: The Strategic Planning Institute, 1983.

Strebel, Paul. *Breakpoints: How Managers Exploit Radical Business Change*. Boston: Harvard Business School Press, 1992.

"Stuck! How Companies Cope When They Can't Raise Prices." *Business Week*, November 15, 1993, pp. 146–155.

Stuckey, M. M. *Demassing: Transforming the Dinosaur Corporation*. Cambridge, Mass.: Productivity Press, 1993.

Summers, Diane. "Corporate Zits Beware." *The Financial Times*, April 14, 1994, p. 9.

Tanner, L. D. "Seeking a Pay Formula." *Monthly Labor Review*, vol. 115, no. 3, March 1992, p. 42.

Tapscott, Don, and Art Caston. *Paradigm Shift: The New Promise of Information Technology*. New York: McGraw-Hill, 1993.

Taylor, Paul. "Benchmark Is Set by Clear Winners in Product Groups." *The Financial Times*, June 27, 1994, p. 9.

Tichy, Noel, and Ram Charan. "Speed, Simplicity, Self-Confidence: An Interview With Jack Welch." *Harvard Business Review*, September–October 1989, pp. 112–120.

Tomasko, Robert M. *Downsizing: Reshaping the Corporation for the Future*. New York: AMACOM, 1990.

————. *Rethinking the Corporation: The Architecture of Change*. New York: AMACOM, 1993.

Tully, Shawn. "The Real Key to Creating Wealth." *Fortune*, September 22, 1993, pp. 38–52.

————. "Raiding a Company's Hidden Cash. " *Fortune*, vol. 130, no. 4, August 22, 1994, pp. 82–89.

Uchitelle, Louis. "The New Faces of U.S. Manufacturing." *The New York Times,* July 3, 1994, pp. 3–1, 3–6.

Utterback, James. *Mastering the Dynamics of Innovation: How Companies Can Seize Opportunities in the Face of Technological Change.* Boston: Harvard Business School Press, 1994.

Von Oech, Roger. *A Whack on the Side of the Head.* New York: Warner Books, 1990.

Walther, George R. *Upside-Down Marketing.* New York: McGraw Hill, 1994.

Walton, Sam, with John Huey. *Sam Walton: Made in America.* New York: Doubleday, 1992).

Waterman, Robert H., Jr. *The Renewal Factor: How the Best Get and Keep the Competitive Edge.* New York: Bantam Books, 1987.

———. *Adhocracy.* New York: W. W. Norton, 1992.

———. *What America Does Right: Learning From Corporations That Put People First.* New York: W. W. Norton, 1994.

Watson, Gregory H. *The Benchmarking Workbook: Adapting Best Practices for Performance Improvement.* Cambridge, Mass.: Productivity Press, 1992.

———. *Strategic Benchmarking: How to Rate Your Company's Performance Against the World's Best.* New York: Wiley, 1993.

Wayland, Robert E. "Customer Valuation: The Foundation of Customer Franchise Management." *Mercer Management Journal,* no. 2, 1994, pp. 45–57.

Wendel, Charles. "Behind the Management Buzzwords." *American Banker,* November 29, 1993.

———. "Four Sharp Tools for Learning How Your Bank Measures Up." *American Banker,* September 27, 1993.

Wenner, David, and Richard W. LeBer. "Managing for Shareholder Value—From Top to Bottom," *Harvard Business Review,* November–December 1989, pp. 52–66.

Whitney, John O. *The Trust Factor: Liberating Profits & Restoring Corporate Vitality.* New York: McGraw-Hill, 1993.

Wired Magazine, a monthly publication of Wired USA Ltd., 544 Second Street, San Francisco, Calif. 94107-1427.

Womack, James P., and Daniel T. Jones. "From Lean Production to the Lean Enterprise." *Harvard Business Review,* March–April 1994, pp. 93–103.

Womack, J. P., D. T. Jones, and D. Ross. *The Machine That Changed the World.* New York: Rawson Associates, 1990.

Yergin, Daniel, and Thane Gustafson. *Russia 2010: And What It Means for the World.* New York: Random House, 1994.

Zellner, Wendy, and Andrea Rothman. "The Airline Mess." *Business Week,* July 6, 1993, p. 50.

Zuboff, Shoshana. *In the Age of the Smart Machine: The Future of Work and Power.* New York: BasicBooks, 1988.

Index